OUTDOOR PIG PRODUCTION

By the same author
Practical Pig Production

OUTDOOR PIG PRODUCTION

KEITH THORNTON

FARMING PRESS LIMITED
Wharfedale Road, Ipswich, Suffolk IP1 4LG

First published 1988

British Library Cataloguing in Publication Data
Thornton, Keith
Outdoor pig production.
1. Livestock : Pigs. Production
I. Title
636.4

ISBN 0-85236-178-5

Distributed in North America by Diamond Farm Enterprises,
Box 537, Alexandria Bay, NY 13607

Phototypeset by Galleon Photosetting, Ipswich
Printed in Great Britain at Butler and Tanner, Frome, Somerset

Contents

page
PREFACE   xiii

1. INTRODUCTION   1

Historical perspective: ancient times – eighteenth century and afterwards – modern times. Traditional outdoor production in the United Kingdom: advantages of the outdoor pig herd – disadvantages. Outdoor pig production overseas: United States of America – China. Recent changes in pig production in the United Kingdom: capital costs – operating costs – countryside policies – recent technical changes. Conclusions.

2. BASIC ESSENTIALS AND POLICY DECISIONS   18

Basic essentials: environment – breeding policy – health – feeding and nutrition – management systems, recording and staff – marketing – financial planning. Summary of basic policy decisions.

3. THE SYSTEM, HOUSING, FENCING AND EQUIPMENT   32

The system: arable rotation – owned or rented ground – choice of management system – land requirements and stocking density – integration with the arable farm – grassland terms. Layout of paddocks: 480 sow requirements – 100 sow requirements – 60 sow requirements – radial paddock layout. Service tracks and access areas. Housing, fencing and equipment: pig housing – fencing – vehicles – other facilities and storage – water supply and equipment. Weaner housing: weaner arks – the Trobridge weaner unit.

4. FEEDING   54

Current recommendations for indoor sows. Special considerations for outdoor sows: fat reserves – group system – outdoor gilts – boars – compound feeds – grazing – straw intake – arable residues. Storage, distribution and feeding methods: bulk or bag – distribution – feeding methods. Feeding patterns: climatic conditions – grazing or stubble available – sow conditions – diet specification – gilts – weaner gilts – creep feeding – feeding the weaner. Total feed amounts.

v

5. MANAGEMENT 65

Some assumptions: location – herd size – weaning – replacements – staff – health – finance. Setting up the new herd: introduction – checklist. Management of breeding stock at critical stages: weaning – weaning to service – gestation – farrowing – gilts – weaner gilts – boars. Management of the weaner: management – post-weaning guidelines and targets.

6. BREEDING POLICY 81

Main objectives: sow productivity – economy of gain – suitability of carcase for the selected market. Objectives applied to outdoor pig production: females – boars. Review of breeds: British Saddleback – Hampshire – Large White – British Landrace – Duroc. Cross-breeding system. Choice of replacement breeding stock: home-bred replacements – purchasing all replacement parent gilts and boars – replacement rates – artificial insemination. Sources of breeding stock.

7. LABOUR AND STAFFING 95

Requirements for outdoor stockmen: stockmanship and pig husbandry – concern for stock welfare – knowledge of the system – outdoor environment – physical fitness – decision making – teamwork – knowledge of machinery and equipment – recording of physical performance – family support. The employer: provide a suitable framework – indicate specific requirements – targets – physical needs – time off – broader horizons – rewards – family support – job satisfaction – performance review. Indoors or outdoors? Number of staff. Training on the farm – Agricultural Training Board – agricultural colleges.

8. SOME HEALTH CONSIDERATIONS 102

Positive health control. The role of veterinary adviser: setting up or expanding a unit – site location – sources of breeding stock – integration and acclimatisation – herd visits – back-up service – vaccination programme. Integration and acclimatisation: background to disease levels – immunity – methods. Herd health programme: vaccination programme – parasite control. Management and health interactions: lameness and injury – heatstroke and sunburn – seasonal infertility – vices. The drug and veterinary store.

9. RECORDING, BUDGETS AND RESULTS 121

Recording: for outdoor pig production – choice of system – Pigtales. Production records, budgets and financial planning: financial planning – preparing budgets – financial comparisons – capital costs – gross margin budget for outdoor herds. Results for outdoor herds: comparison of outdoor and indoor breeding herds – financial results for outdoor herds.

10. CURRENT DEVELOPMENTS AND A FORWARD LOOK 158

Management systems: electronic sow feeding and indoor service. Housing and equipment. Feeding. Current developments overseas. A forward look – a role for the Duroc breed?

APPENDICES

I   *Cash flows (60 and 480 sow modules)*   168
II *Conversion tables*   188
III *Suppliers*   192
IV *Background reading*   198

INDEX   201

Plates

		page
1	Richard Roadnight	23
2	Large White boar	26
3	Saddleback sow	30
4	Group of Duroc gilts	38
5	Group of Camborough Blues	38
6	Sows outdoors in farrowing paddocks	39
7	Group of Duroc cross White sows	40
8	Landrace boars	47
9	Radial lay-out	62
10	Farrowing paddocks	62
11	Inspection of farrowing hut	74
12	Chopped straw blown into farrowing hut	74
13	Farrow hut and fender	74
14	Metal fender	88
15	Double farrowing huts	88
16	Boar ark	89
17	Dry sow ark in gestation paddock	89
18	Sows in gestation paddock	112
19	Sows inspecting wallow bath	112
20	Lactating sows	113
21	Home made water drinker	113
22	Paddock gateway	126
23	Home made location board	126
24	Water tanker	127
25	Portable tool kit	127
26	Terrain vehicle	142
27	Service vehicle	142
28	Newly weaned sows	143
29	Group of sows outside electronic feeding station	163
30	Weaner bungalows	163
31	Group of newly weaned outdoor pigs	165
32	Straw yard system	165

Figures

		page
1.1	The proportion of sows in different herd sizes in Great Britain	4
1.2	The distribution of weaning ages, 1980 and 1986	14
1.3	Entire males as a percentage of total pig classifications, 1977–86	14
2.1	Average rainfall, Britain and Ireland	20
2.2	Main rock and soil types, Great Britain	21
3.1	Typical production cycle for outdoor herds	34
3.2	Pig flow through the paddocks, 480–500 sow outdoor unit	36
3.3	Pig flow through a 100 sow unit	42
3.4	60 sow unit	42
3.5	Radial paddock layout	44
4.1	Suggested sow feeding profile	61
5.1	The twice-weekly weaning system	70
5.2	Management and feeding recommendations for maiden and weaner gilts	76
6.1	The closed herd multiplier	90
6.2	Purchasing replacement females as parents	92
8.1	Combined management and veterinary appraisal	106
9.1	Ear notching	123
9.2	Bureau-based computerised recording system	128
9.3	Pigtales diary card	129
9.4	Pigtales weekly report	131
9.5	Pigtales sow card	132
9.6	Pigtales special analysis report	133
9.7	Pigtales quarterly analysis	134
9.8	A pathway to financial planning	136

Tables

		page
1.1	Changes in operating costs	11
1.2	Trends in weaning age	16
4.1	Effect of feeding level after weaning-to-oestrus period in primiparous sows	58
4.2	Interaction between feed intake in pregnancy and lactation.	59
4.3	Summary of sow and gilt feeding patterns	63
6.1	Individual and maternal heterosis	86
8.1	Effects of changing parameters on the theoretical profit of a pig farm	104
9.1	Financial results for weaner producers	139
9.2	Costs for weaner production as a percentage of net output	140
9.3	Results for outdoor breeding herds	147
9.4	Results for breeding herds farrowing outdoors	148
9.5	Comparison of outdoor and indoor breeding herds	149
9.6	Results for outdoor and indoor herds, June 1986	150
9.7	Comparison of outdoor and indoor herds (Cambridge Pig Management Scheme)	151
9.8	Outdoor and indoor herds (Exeter Pig Recording Schemes)	153
9.9	Outdoor herds – financial results (MLC)	155
9.10	Gross margins for weaner producers	156
9.11	Gross margins for breeding and feeding herds	157

Acknowledgements

IN THE preparation and writing of the book I have had help and advice from many people and organisations in the industry. I frequently turned to my former colleagues in PIC for information; in particular to Dr Maurice Bichard, Tony Brown and Keith Poulson. Hannah Kilgour, Projects Manager, was always adept at digging out references and special requests. My thanks also to PIC for permission to use photographs, illustrations and their specimen cash flow. Eric Oates of Peninsular Pigs (SW) and Nigel Handscombe of Masterbreeders also kindly allowed me to use photographs, information, diagrams and cash-flow information from their company literature. The National Pig Breeders Association also provided background information on the various breeds.

Specific comments and helpful advice came from John Chalmers of ADAS in Bristol and from David Allott in Reading. Andrew Shepherd of the Agricultural Economics Unit of Exeter University also provided information and background from the Exeter Reports.

The MLC *Year Book* now provides the industry with important facts and figures and I am grateful to Mike Potter and Len Croft for their help and interpretation in this area. Mick Hazzledine of Dalgety Agriculture also answered my queries on some aspects of feeding and nutrition. Ted Nelson MRCVS of the Larkmead Veterinary Group read through the first draft of my chapter on Health Considerations and made a number of helpful comments and observations. I would like to thank the Pig Veterinary Society for permission to use diagrams and illustrations from their *Proceedings*. I have referred to their publications on a number of occasions.

Photographs have been supplied from a number of sources to whom I am grateful. These include Miss M. G. Roadnight (plate 1), *Pig Farming* magazine, Profort Farms (plates 15, 16), Pig Breeders Supply Company (plate 30), Arthur Shepherd, Gallagher Agricultural Ltd, Europe (plate 21) and Ian and Gillian Bossinger from Kentucky in the United States (plate 6). Gerry Brent allowed me to xii

use his diagram from the *Pigman's Handbook* on ear notching. The pen and ink drawing for the frontispiece was kindly provided by Seren Bell.

I would also like to thank John Goss of Tubney in Oxfordshire and Alec Jones of Extensive Management Services, Black Bourton, Oxon. They both allowed me to spend some time working on their outdoor units, to get my hands dirty, to take some photographs and answer my questions. My visit to the Jones farm coincided with a sharp spell of frost so I was privileged to operate the water bowser.

Finally thanks to my wife Shirley and daughter Gillian who have been able to interpret my handwriting and prepared the typed script, and to Martin Looker and Roger Smith, of *Pig Farming* magazine and Farming Press Books, for their encouragement, help and guidance.

Preface

SINCE 1978 I have been living overseas and working in two important but very different centres of pig production. For almost eight years my main base was the Mid-West region of the United States which was followed by a challenging period managing a contract in Guangzhou in the People's Republic of China.

Throughout this period I was able to maintain contact with the United Kingdom industry through my PIC colleagues, from many visitors from home and through *Pig Farming* magazine and other technical publications. Producers in most parts of the world still look towards the United Kingdom for information and new developments in all aspects of pig production. British breeds and technology have an important role in world pigmeat production, and new ideas and methods continue to emerge which have widespread application in many countries.

On my return to live in England in 1987 I was able to catch up first hand with a number of significant changes that were taking place in the United Kingdom industry.

Clearly defined structural changes continue, with a relatively static number of breeding sows in the national herd but now reduced to a hard core of about four thousand breeding herds containing about eighty per cent of all sows. I noticed an increasing concern and emphasis on meat quality with a small but encouraging increase in pigmeat consumption to over 21.0 kg per head in 1986.

There is clear evidence that animal welfare considerations have an increasing influence on many aspects of pig farming, and pigmeat production. One other remarkable feature was the growth and development of outdoor pig production. Published results indicated that production compared favourably with indoor intensive systems and were being achieved with much lower capital costs and with a combination of traditional methods and new ideas.

Successful outdoor production still depends to a large extent on suitable choice of land, a favourable climate and expert stockmanship. At present there is little written factual information on outdoor pig production. In this book I have attempted to bring together existing material from a large number of sources and add to it some objective practical information gathered from a number of successful outdoor producers.

Not everyone will agree with my approach, presentation and analysis of the current situation. Fortunately, as with most aspects of livestock production, there is lots of room for disagreement. I hope the book will be of interest to existing producers, and will be instructive to other potential outdoor producers. It seems certain that outdoor pig systems will be an important and significant feature of pig production in the United Kingdom, and in a number of other countries in other parts of the world.

Somerset 1988

KEITH THORNTON

Chapter One

INTRODUCTION

HISTORICAL PERSPECTIVE

PIG PRODUCTION since the domestication of the pig has historically been based on keeping the breeding sow out of doors, or at least partially out of doors. Over the years, the pig was gradually moved indoors by way of the cottager's sty. This eventually led to the development of the full confinement systems for both breeding and feeding herds which now account for the great part of the pig industry.

Ancient Times

From a historical perspective the pig has been a scavenger, living and foraging in forests, woods and orchards. In Britain, according to legend, the keeping of large herds of pigs out of doors can be traced back to the middle of the ninth century BC.

At the time of the Domesday Book the right of 'pannage', or running of pigs in the manorial woods, was a valuable privilege. Pigs fed on acorns, beech mast, bracken, ferns, roots, fruit and seeds from a wide range of vegetation.

Domestic pig production probably did not change very much until the eighteenth century, with the enclosure of land and the first major increase in human population.

Eighteenth Century and Afterwards

During the Industrial Revolution of the eighteenth century there was a dramatic increase in the growth of the urban population and at the same time a need to feed this population. In this situation there was less space for the pig out of doors, which led to the first steps towards confinement. The pig was often confined in areas adjacent to its food supply, which may have been of domestic, agricultural or industrial origin. A good example of this is illustrated

1

by the building of the cottager's sty for the utilisation of domestic and household waste, supplemented by home-grown vegetables and root crops.

Growth in the pig population also took place in areas where cereals—mainly barley and oats—were produced. East Anglia, Yorkshire and the South-eastern counties in England provide good examples of this. The availability of agricultural and industrial by-products also influenced the location of pig production. Whey and skim milk, which were by-products of cheese manufacturing, led to growth of pig production in Cheshire and the Fylde district of Lancashire, as well as in the South-western counties. Another major feed source for pigs in confinement was provided by the alcoholic drinks industry.

Distillers' waste consisted of the spent grains and wash produced when extracting spirits. Brewery waste was spent grains alone, now called brewer's grain. These waste products were used as a supply of feedingstuffs for cattle and pigs, and made a major contribution to the provisioning and feeding of eighteenth-century London.

Estimates of the number of pigs involved vary enormously, but over a hundred thousand were fattened annually in the middle of the century. It was a seasonal business as the brewing industry only operated from October until May. Store pigs were driven on foot from counties as far afield as Yorkshire, Shropshire, Berkshire and Leicestershire to the main market at Finchley on the outskirts of north London. After harvest the brewers wanted lean store pigs, which were about fifteen months old. They were able to fatten these on grain and wash without the addition of beans or peas. Some brewers were then able to sell their fat pigs, through valuable victualling contracts, direct to the Royal Navy.

Farmers complained bitterly about the quality of these industrial pigs and the undercutting of their traditional markets. Graziers were unable to compete with the brewers as they had to collect their pigs from around the countryside and drive them long distances to ports, the pigs losing condition on the way.

This early story of entrepreneurship, integration, hogwash and chicanery in the marketplace has a familiar and contemporary ring about it!

Industrial by-products from sugar refining, flour milling, biscuit- and bread-making were also available and widely used, mainly on the edge of towns and cities since transport facilities were not well developed. The availability of cereals, milk and industrial by-products strongly influenced the distribution of pigs at the end of the nineteenth century and the beginning of the twentieth century, and had a strong bearing on the pattern and distribution of the pig industry today.

Modern Times

The move to the cereal-producing areas of the Eastern Counties did not take place until after the First World War, but the pattern is discernible when we look at records for the mid 1920s. This period also witnessed the development of the first confinement buildings with the adaptation of the Danish-type building for fattening pigs. At the same time the animal feed compound business developed with the growth of the port mills, such as Liverpool and Bristol, which imported maize, barley and wheat from North America. Improved road and rail systems facilitated the transportation of animal feeds to farms throughout the country. In this way, the current pattern of pig production was fashioned and the distribution was stabilised on a regional basis still evident today.

After the Second World War the end of animal feed rationing was followed by a period of expansion in pig production to satisfy the increasing demand for pigmeat products, which had been in short supply during and immediately after the war. From 1954 onwards the emphasis in pig production moved increasingly towards specialisation, with a move towards confinement at all stages of production. In this period of twenty to twenty-five years, pigs moved almost wholly indoors into very specialist buildings. Sows farrowed in crates with supplementary heating for young pigs. Breeding sows were housed in yards with individual feeders, which eventually led to individual sow stalls and tether systems. Weaners, growers and fattening pigs were housed in insulated buildings, frequently fitted with mechanical ventilation. Increased stocking rates and a desire to remove the drudgery and physical effort involved in manure removal led to the development of slatted floor systems and the handling of manure in a liquid form. The move towards economy of feed usage and better utilisation of labour made for increasing demands on capital investment in specialist pig production. By the beginning of the 1970s the pig industry was becoming increasingly specialised, with fewer and larger units accounting for a large share of the total output (see figure 1.1).

By 1980, the British industry could be considered to be operating on a high-cost basis but with high outputs, and leading the world in the application of technology and in technical developments. The economics of the industry left no room for the inefficient, and

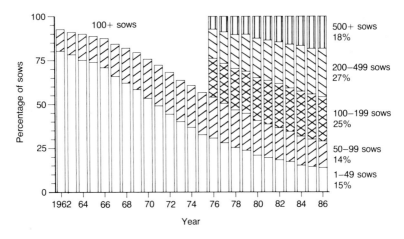

Figure 1.1   The proportion of sows in different herd sizes in Great Britain.
Source: Pig Improvement Company.

potential new entrants were faced with massive capital investment if they were to be successful in this very specialist business.

TRADITIONAL OUTDOOR PRODUCTION IN THE UNITED KINGDOM

This brief, personal and historical review of pig production in the United Kingdom is important. It puts into perspective the resurgence of outdoor pig production, because not all producers followed the trend towards confinement already described.

The system of large-scale outdoor pig-keeping was developed by Mr Richard Roadnight on his farm at Britwell Salome near Watlington in Oxfordshire. Present-day methods depend largely on the sound principles he practised and popularised amongst a small group of pioneers. In the 1950s he was growing barley as the main crop on his 2,500 acre (1,000 hectare) farm, with a grass break in the rotation carrying a sheep flock. His search for an alternative break crop led to a decision to try an outdoor herd of breeding sows. The choice of breed was the Saddleback, chosen for its strong maternal instincts, together with sufficient hardiness to stand up to outdoor conditions, as well as its ability to use waste grain and sugar beet tops, and to graze without excessive supplementation with compound feed. Eventually the breeding system was based on crossing the Saddleback with a Landrace boar producing the 'Britwell Blue', which proved to be an excellent female for the outdoor breeding herd.

The system was based on a relatively large herd of four hundred sows which would farrow twice a year in March and September. This programme of spring and autumn farrowing allowed the young pigs to avoid the worst of the winter weather. The March-born pigs could be sold off the field as strong stores later in the year, and September-born litters could be moved on to be fattened in straw yards.

Weaning would take place between eight and ten weeks of age, when all the litters could be rounded up and sorted. The weaned sows would then be put back to the boars for service. The system worked extremely well and was regarded as a low-cost and low-output system. Sow productivity measured in terms of pigs weaned per sow per year, for this outdoor system, would fall in the range of twelve to fourteen.

Major drawbacks at that time included laborious methods of paddock fencing with stakes, pig netting and barbed wire. Costs of fencing were high so paddocks were often large, holding large groups of sows but with a relatively low stocking rate of five or six sows per hectare.

The system demanded a large number of boars to cope with the twice-yearly farrowing pattern, and barren sows and sows returning to service proved difficult to fit into the routine, depressing the overall performance. Success depended on dedicated stockmanship, use of light, free-draining land, and market outlets that at that time did not penalise fairly generous levels of backfat in the progeny.

The Roadnight system, and variations on it, were widely adopted in various parts of the United Kingdom, especially in the southern counties of England, and as far north as Aberdeen. In the late 1960s several large outdoor pig units could be seen directly under the flight path as the landing approach was made to Aberdeen airport.

Outdoor pig-keeping had also developed in other parts of the United Kingdom but on more traditional lines. These herds tended to be in the south and east of the country with large concentrations of pigs in East Anglia, especially the counties of Cambridgeshire, Suffolk and Norfolk. Herds were generally smaller than those following the Roadnight system, and in some cases herds were not kept out of doors all the year round. On some farms movable arks and folds could be drawn on to a concrete slab for the winter period, with electricity and water laid on. Large straw-bedded yards were also used for groups of sows during gestation in winter. These herds would often graze cereal stubbles and sometimes clean up after root crops. Tethering of sows out of doors, with sows attached to a spike in the ground by a 35 foot (12 metre) chain, had virtually disappeared, mainly because of demands on labour for moving sows to fresh ground, but also because of lack of control of young pigs.

Most of these sows running out of doors, or partially out of doors, were 'blue' sows, usually a cross between the Saddleback and Landrace breeds. Occasionally the Welsh or Large White breeds were used as alternatives to the Landrace and, in some areas, the Large Black found favour. Overall, the 'Blue' sow formed the basis of the sow herd and the usual choice of boar used to produce the slaughter generation was Large White, followed by the Landrace.

Outdoor units were established in Hampshire, Wiltshire, Dorset, Kent, Essex, Oxfordshire and Buckinghamshire, and information on these herds can be found in a *Report on an Economic Investigation of Outdoor Pig Production*, published by M. A. Boddington of the School of Rural Economics and Related Studies, Wye College, London, in 1971. This followed survey work carried out by Wye College and the Department of Agricultural Economics, Reading University, in 1968 and 1969. This very comprehensive report covered:

- Results of a postal survey.
- Financial and physical results in the outdoor pig herd.
- Some characteristics of outdoor pig herds and farms.
- Outdoor pigs as a break crop.
- Summary and conclusions.

The report summarised the advantages of the outdoor pig herd as follows:

Advantages of the Outdoor Pig Herd

The outdoor herd has many attractive features to recommend it. Some of the more important ones are:

1. Profitability compares very favourably with the indoor herd.
2. Strong healthy store pigs are produced, for which there is good demand.
3. Labour costs are lower than for the indoor herd.
4. There is no slurry problem.
5. Capital outlay is low.

Disadvantages of the Outdoor Pig Herd

Whilst there are considerable drawbacks in the outdoor herd, these are often offset by the advantages. Drawbacks to the enterprise include:

1. Productivity tends to be low.
2. It is hard to manage individual animals, and controlling pigs is not easy.
3. Barren sows and sterile boars may be carried for some time before they are recognised.
4. The enterprise is generally restricted to light land.
5. Fencing requirements may be heavy and sows may not respect the fences.
6. Mud can be a major problem in winter.
7. Visiting pigs on outlying land may be difficult, especially in winter.
8. Foxes may take young pigs, and birds and vermin will almost certainly steal food.

These are the broad conclusions which summarise the advantages and disadvantages of a number of different types of outdoor pig production at the beginning of the 1970s. Later in this chapter I shall return to examine outdoor pig-keeping in 1988, and see how the situation and circumstances have changed.

OUTDOOR PIG PRODUCTION OVERSEAS

A brief look at a few pig-producing countries overseas illustrates that a similar pattern has been followed in a wide range of countries. Traditionally, the pig was the forager and scavenger, and did not become confined into intensive systems until the first half of the twentieth century.

United States of America

Pig production is now concentrated in the Corn Belt states of the Mid-West, but this was not always the case. Pigs emigrated from Europe to the Americas through the Caribbean with the early pioneers in the fifteenth and sixteenth centuries, and quickly made themselves at home.

The woodlands and hills along the Atlantic seaboard were similar to those of Europe. Pigs were mostly confined in towns, but ranged the woods and grazed the land, and escaped to lead a feral existence. British pigs arrived with the early colonists in the New England States, spread to the Mid-Atlantic colonies and eventually to Pennsylvania, which became the great hog colony in the second half of the nineteenth century.

The real advance in American pig production took place in the first half of the nineteenth century, as the settlers moved west and took their pigs with them. The pigs which trekked into the unexplored territories with the frontiersmen were basically 'wood' pigs, because they were able to feed by foraging in the woods and forests. By the mid nineteenth century the United States' pig population was over ten million, or roughly half the human population at that time. The route to the West lay through Ohio, and Cincinnati was an early centre of slaughtering and processing. By the early nineteenth century, the geographical spread was centred on the Corn Belt states of Iowa, Illinois, Indiana, Ohio, Missouri, Nebraska, Kansas and Michigan. Chicago then became 'pork butcher to the world'. These states accounted for over half of the United States' output of pigmeat, and with only a few changes the pattern was established for the present-day distribution of pig production in the United States.

The management system by the 1940s was based on twice-yearly farrowing in March and September, or spring and fall. Farrowing took place in portable wooden huts or arks and, during gestation, groups of sows ran out at pasture or on the ground in 'dirt lots'. The breeding programme was based on the three-breed rotational crossing system, using the Yorkshire, Duroc and Hampshire breeds. The progeny were fed ad-lib to market weight in partially enclosed yards on home-grown corn, and quite often in dirt lots out of doors. Herds were frequently turned out in the autumn to graze and forage in vast acres of maize stubble. The geographical location of the Corn Belt leads to extreme variations in climatic conditions with exceptionally cold, snowy winters and hot humid summers.

The challenging climate and increasing demand for pigmeat products paved the way for a major move towards intensification of pig production in the 1960s. Many new confinement units were built which would most likely have a slatted floor system, automatic ventilation and mechanical feeding. Not all producers followed this pattern, but intensification was widely adopted in Nebraska, Northern Iowa, Minnesota, Illinois and Indiana. In slightly milder climates Missouri and Southern Illinois have retained some of their outdoor systems. In recent years, the state of North Carolina has become a major producer of pigmeat. The favourable climate to some extent offsets the extra cost of importing corn from the Mid-West States. Whilst North Carolina has a number of intensive units with sows kept indoors, there are a large number of outdoor producers. The climate and soil types found there probably lend themselves to outdoor pig production on similar lines to developments in the United Kingdom. The likely areas for an expansion of outdoor production include the Carolinas, Kentucky, Tennessee, Georgia and Arkansas.

Many other changes have taken place in the American hog industry in recent years, with transfer of technological and husbandry methods from the United Kingdom including continuous farrowing, earlier weaning and the widespread use of European white cross-bred females, as well as improved methods of recording.

In 1987, the United States' industry had about 6.3 million sows. The trend, as in Europe, is toward fewer, more specialist farms and the number of farms is halving every fourteen years. Nearly all producers buy in boars and about 15 to 20 per cent buy in replacement breeding gilts. Approximately three-quarters of producers sell their finished hogs on a liveweight basis at about 109 to 115 kg liveweight. American consumers are increasingly concerned about cholesterol levels and animal fat in their diet, which may eventually affect methods of production through the market.

On balance, and probably due to the wide range of geographical locations and the many variations in climatic conditions, the United States' industry keeps proportionately more pigs out of doors than does the United Kingdom industry. United States' producers and advisers are watching with great interest recent developments in outdoor pig production in England, and will be ready to adopt them in similar locations and conditions.

China

The Peoples' Republic of China (PRC) is the world's largest pig-keeper, and provides enormous contrast to both United States and European pig production. PRC is a vast country with a population of around one billion people, the great majority of them living in rural areas and mainly involved in obtaining a living from the land. Pigmeat provides over 90 per cent of the meat supply for their diet, with fish the main alternative. To provide this enormous population with their staple meat supply, the PRC has an estimated twenty-one million sows, with a total of over three hundred million pigs in the national inventory at any one time. In contrast, the inventory estimates for the United States would be about fifty million and for West Germany around 22.5 million pigs.

Traditionally in the PRC pigs were raised and kept in self-sufficient peasant smallholdings, with each family raising only enough for its own consumption. Things are changing slowly, with a move towards small-scale commercial production in specialised households, but still with only a few sows in each household. Some recent figures from the Chinese Academy of Agricultural Sciences report over 7.2 million farms, with one or two sows each. These are the sows that the visitor to China will see the length and breadth of the country. There are many breeds of pigs, which are comparatively small by Western standards with a dipped back and hanging belly. They are to be found wandering around the villages, with a litter not too far away, foraging for any spare food that is available. Their main diet will be made up from a wide range of vegetables, including varieties of cabbage and roots, supplemented by household waste. Agricultural by-products from food processing, sericulture (silkworm breeding) and flour and rice milling also provide a source of pig feed.

There are a few larger commercial units being developed in the PRC. This is in line with the national policy of Lean Pork Production, which is an integral part of the current seventh Five Year Plan (1986–1990). Many of these larger commercial units are located in east and south coast provinces which have direct access to the Hong Kong market for export of live meat pigs at about 100 kg liveweight. Most of these pigs are railed direct to Hong Kong and earn valuable foreign exchange, but this specialist export market is strictly controlled by a well-established quota system. The great bulk of pigmeat in China will continue, at least for the next few years, to be produced by a combination of peasant farmers and specialised households. It can in no way be described as outdoor pig production in the accepted Western sense, but provides an interesting contrast to methods of pig production in other parts of the world.

RECENT CHANGES IN PIG PRODUCTION IN THE UNITED KINGDOM

How have circumstances changed in the United Kingdom to lead, in the last six to ten years, to a revival in outdoor pig production? All sections of the pig industry have been under a great deal of pressure for many years, and economic forces have been instrumental in bringing change and the adoption of new techniques and ideas. Some developments in the indoor industry have helped to transform the traditional methods of outdoor pig production and must be considered against this background of changing circumstances.

Capital Costs

The capital cost of building new confinement housing for pigs has risen dramatically in the past few years. The capital cost may be as high as £1,200 to £1,500 per sow place. Pig housing and equipment do not qualify for any financial support or grant aid. Servicing of capital repayment and interest charges may place prohibitively high costs against any new investment. This can be illustrated by figures over a twenty-year period from the University of Exeter Pig Cost Survey.

In 1964/65 capital costs per sow for an indoor breeding herd were £28 per sow. By 1974/75 this figure had risen to £96 per sow and by 1984/85 had reached £412. Allowing for inflation, with corrected figures based on 1984/85, the value for each of the years quoted would be £177, £311 and £412 respectively. Other University and Meat and Livestock Commission figures indicate a similar rising trend in capital investment for indoor pig housing. Current estimates of costs for housing and equipment of an outdoor system are in the range from £150 to £180 per sow, a significant difference. An additional cost must of course be attributed to the value of the land occupied by the outdoor pigs.

Operating Costs

Feed has always been the major cost of pig production, but in recent years there have been increases in labour and other costs relative to feed costs. There have been notable reductions in labour usage per sow, but at the same time there have been rapid increases in the cost of labour. With a move towards earlier weaning, extra fuel and electricity may be needed, and the charges for these services have moved ahead of inflation. A glance at comparative costs of indoor and outdoor pig enterprises quickly highlights the extra costs incurred by indoor pigs in labour, electricity, gas and repairs and maintenance to buildings.

Table 1.1 Changes in operating costs

| | % COSTS | | |
	Feed	Other Costs	Total Costs
63/64	84.4	15.6	100
75/76	77.5	22.5	100
85/86	71.0	29.0	100

The situation is best summarised by a statement from the University of Exeter Agricultural Economics Unit *Report on Pig Production in South West England in 1985/86*. 'It will come as no surprise, then, to learn that for the Breeding Feeding herds, labour and other costs changed.' Their results are shown in table 1.1.

Countryside Politics

The growth and operation of large-scale intensive farming systems has become a sensitive issue in the countryside in the 1980s. Dairy, pig and poultry operations have grown in size and scale, with a large number of animals housed in confined areas. These farms are an essential part of the agricultural economy and are making a valuable contribution by producing a wide range of high-quality foods at very competitive prices. However, against a background of over-production of some commodities, demands by the public for greater access to the countryside, and an increasing concern about the way in which farm animals are kept, the farmer has to pick his way very carefully through existing legislation and changing attitudes and concerns.

The large-scale pig producer faces a number of difficult areas including:

1. Planning Regulations.
2. Storage and Spreading of Farm Waste.
3. Animal Welfare.

Legislation and recommendations in these areas will shape how farm animals are kept in the future.

Most pig producers are well aware of these issues. They have modified their approach where necessary and apply good stockmanship with a sympathetic attitude towards animal husbandry. Many of the contentious areas can be resolved and the great bulk of pig production will continue to come from indoor production and intensive systems.

One other relevant issue faces those cereal growers who have become efficient at growing corn with high yields but with high fertiliser usage and high costs. Under EEC regulations they are now faced with a co-responsibility levy of £3.40 per tonne. In reassessing their position, do they leave some of their land fallow or turn to alternative enterprises? Feeding some of their home-grown cereals to progeny from an outdoor herd which will also provide a break in the arable rotation is a proposition worthy of consideration.

Recent Technical Changes in the Pig Industry

Against this background, a number of other changes have been taking place in the pig industry in the last ten years. Some have been brought about by economic pressures, others through the adoption of research and technology, and some through changes in the market and consumer demands. These changes have been widely absorbed throughout the United Kingdom pig industry, but some are of specific interest to the large-scale outdoor pig producer.

Earlier Weaning

The trend in the industry over the past ten years has been towards earlier weaning. A move towards weaning at between three and four weeks of age has been of significant benefit to outdoor pig production. Most producers do not now creep feed, and suckling pigs can be confined inside the farrowing hut until they are weaned. This reduces daily labour demands for servicing litters, eliminates creep feed losses to birds and vermin, and cuts out the cost and work of cleaning feeders. It also makes for easier handling and catching of pigs. In some cases, weaned pigs can be sold direct from the field, and earlier weaning provides the opportunity to increase sow productivity to more than two litters per sow per year (see Table 1.2 and Figure 1.2).

Regular Farrowing Programme

There has been a move away from twice-yearly farrowing in favour of a regular weekly or monthly programme. With earlier weaning, as already mentioned, sow productivity can be greatly improved,

Table 1.2   Trends in weaning age, 1981–86

Age at weaning (days)	1980	1981	1982	1983	1984	1985	1986
			(Percentage of herds)				
Under 19	5	10	11	8	7	5	3
19–25	41	44	45	54	57	62	67
26–32	13	18	18	19	22	22	21
33–39	32	22	20	15	10	9	7
Over 39	8	6	6	4	3	2	2
No. of herds	653	720	766	739	725	688	711

Source: MLC *Pig Year Book*, 1987.

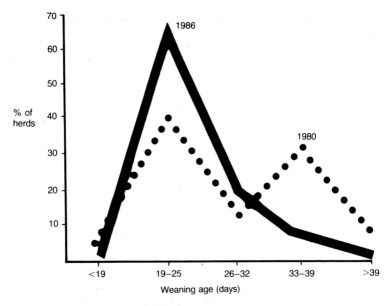

Figure 1.2   The distribution of weaning ages, 1980 and 1986.
Source: MLC *Pig Year Book*, 1987.

Entires as a percentage of total classifications

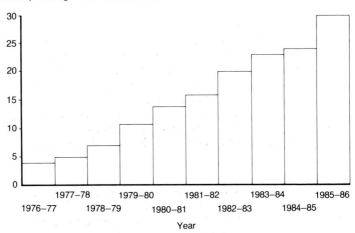

Figure 1.3   Entire males as a percentage of total pig classifications, 1977–86.
Source: MLC *Pig Year Book*, 1987.

and a constant flow of weaners or stores is available for organised marketing. Regular weekly farrowing needs fewer boars than the older twice-yearly farrowing system, and spreads their use throughout the year. Regular farrowing allows the introduction of replacement gilts in a planned manner at appropriate times in the year. Herd size can more easily be maintained, peak demands for labour are lowered, and better use can be made of buildings and equipment. A predictable flow of pigs for regular marketing provides a more stable cash flow than irregular large batches twice a year.

Electric Fencing
Improvements in electric fencing have provided a major breakthrough for the outdoor herd. Modern high-frequency and high-voltage mains, and transistorised battery-operated fences, are efficient in operation, relatively cheap, and are easy to move. Boundary fences, paddocks and gateways can be laid out quickly, and after initial training of gilts, are very effective at keeping breeding stock in place. Smaller paddocks can be tailored for groups of sows and gilts evenly matched according to stage of pregnancy and body condition. Wire netting and barbed wire are no longer required. New approaches and developments continue and new products come on to the market as a number of equipment manufacturers investigate methods of electric fencing for large farm animals.

Entire Boars for Market
Over the past ten years the proportion of entire boars going to slaughter has been steadily increasing. Entire boars grow faster than castrates or gilts, use their feed more efficiently and carry less fat. Approximately two-thirds of all male pigs are now finished as entires. This means that it is no longer necessary to castrate young pigs on outdoor units, which reduces handling and labour requirements. There are marked regional variations and acceptance will depend upon the specific market outlet (see Figure 1.3).

Feed and Water
Animal feed compounders have produced sow feed in physical forms which are very suitable for outdoor systems. This is usually a cob, roll or biscuit, which reduces waste from treading into the mud and is less likely to be carried away by birds. Shy feeders can grab a mouthful and move off to eat in relative peace, away from the more dominant sows. Water can be provided through alkathene pipes,

either on the surface or mole-ploughed in. Modern fittings make jointing, piecing and coupling a relatively simple job.

Supply of Breeding Stock
A number of breeding stock companies and some individual breeders are now offering good-quality gilts which have been specially developed for the outdoor pig producer. These gilts are the result of long-term testing and breed improvement programmes. Backfat levels in the Saddleback breed have been carefully reduced without compromising the hardiness necessary for outdoor sows. This has led to an improvement in the carcase quality and grading of the slaughter generation, when an improved boar is used on the blue hybrid sow. Maiden gilts at 100 kg and weaner gilts at 30 kg are now available, and the market for outdoor breeding stock has become a valuable and competitive one for a number of breeding organisations.

Recording and Identification
The development and adoption of the large flexible plastic ear tag has made animal identification easier than it was with the traditional notching or tattooing methods. This makes for better control of individual animals, even in the large herd, and has led to the use of herd recording systems which have been combined with computerised processing and reporting. There are a number of efficient recording systems on the market, and both Cambridge and Exeter University Pig Management Reports record outdoor herds as a separate category. Outdoor herds were first recorded in the Meat and Livestock Commission *Year Book* in 1979 and are now a regular feature of that report. Whilst the recorded information is of very great interest to the industry from a comparative point of view, the real value lies in the monitoring and management control of the individual breeding herd to meet physical and financial targets.

CONCLUSIONS

These technical advances have removed many of the obstacles to outdoor pig production, and the system can now compete on level terms with farms using more intensive production methods. What was once a low-cost/low-output system has now become a low-cost system with medium to high output. A small group of pioneers has applied a strict business approach to outdoor production, and blended the best of the old traditional systems with some of the best of the new methods currently available.

Much of the background and some of these newer developments are specific to the United Kingdom at the present time. Overseas, the market situation and technical background may be quite different, with great variation in climate and culture, so that the modern version of outdoor pig production may not readily be adapted to all circumstances and all countries. In spite of this, the system will have wide appeal in a number of countries including the United States, France, Spain and the Far East.

Chapter Two

BASIC ESSENTIALS AND POLICY DECISIONS

INTRODUCTION

THE BASIC essentials for successful pig production are now widely recognised and accepted. They apply throughout the world from the technically advanced European countries to the simpler systems of North America, through to some of the more recently established industries in Third World countries. Pig production is an international business. Climates vary, some countries utilise different breeds and crosses, and a variety of consumers in different cultures demand a wide range of pigmeat and pigmeat products. All these factors have a strong influence on the methods and types of production.

BASIC ESSENTIALS

The basic essentials can be summarised under seven main headings:

1. Environment.
2. Breeding policy.
3. Health control.
4. Feeding and nutrition.
5. Management and recording.
6. Marketing of the end product.
7. Financial management and planning.

My intention is to summarise the main requirements for outdoor pig production under these headings and then return to them in more detail in later chapters.

Environment

The environment is a major contributory factor in the success of the outdoor unit. Suitable climatic conditions, with the right sort of land (and well-trained and motivated staff) are undoubtedly the critical ingredients of a successful system.

Climate and Rainfall
Most outdoor units are to be found in the south central and south-western counties of England and in East Anglia. Ideally, annual rainfall should not exceed 30 ins (535 mm) and areas with mild winters are to be preferred; conditions unlikely to be met above a line drawn from the Bristol Channel to The Wash. Sites exposed to high winds should be avoided if possible, but the hurricane-type winds at the end of October 1987 prove that there is no guarantee of protection anywhere. Exposed sites and high winds can lead to huts cartwheeling away, but in humid summer weather some air movement is very welcome.

Soil Type
This is possibly the most important consideration in locating a new unit. Soil should be light and free-draining. Chalk, gravel and sandy soils all meet with approval and are very suitable although sharp flints sometimes associated with chalk soils can cause foot damage. Heavy clay soils should be avoided wherever possible. Muddy paddocks, gateways and access roads can lead to a total failure of the system.

Many of the downland areas in southern England provide ideal conditions and, combined with the mild climate, are good locations for outdoor pig production. Suitable conditions also stretch up from East Anglia, through Nottinghamshire and into Yorkshire.

Topography
Level or gently sloping fields make the best sites. Steeply sloping ground should be avoided for farrowing paddocks, as straw bedding gravitates to the lower end of the huts. Steep slopes can also give problems of access for service vehicles in winter. A balance must be found between soil type and topography, and the higher the rainfall the more unsuitable the site becomes. Land above the 800 ft (240 metre) contour is usually too cold and windy to be suitable.

Services
Mains electricity nearby is an advantage but not essential. A good

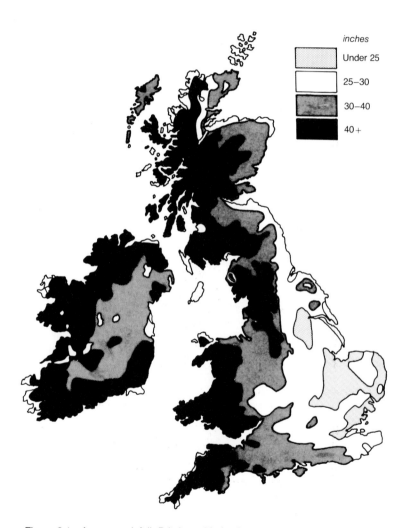

inches

Under 25

25–30

30–40

40+

Figure 2.1   Average rainfall, Britain and Ireland.

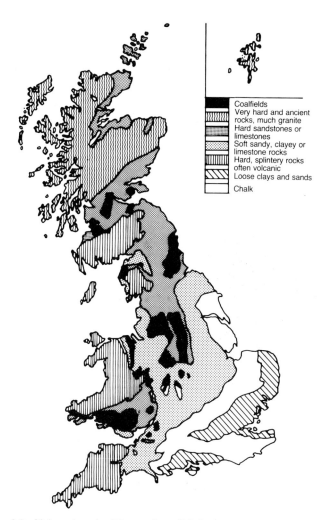

Figure 2.2 Main rock and soil types, Great Britain.

Outdoor pig production presents its own difficulties in the movement of stock and protection from climatic extremes. Two solutions by Emil van Beest (*Pigmania*, Farming Press).

Plate 1   Richard Roadnight and his stockman in front of their Saddleback and 'Britwell Blue' sows, Oxfordshire 1962.

water supply with sufficient pressure to reach all parts of the site is important. The unit should not be too remote from the main farm or staff housing, as this could create a security risk. Rustling of outdoor pigs has occasionally been reported. Public footpaths and bridleways should be avoided as a matter of course. Access by uninvited and unauthorised visitors, who may constitute a disease risk, should be discouraged.

Breeding Policy

There are a number of decisions to make about the breeding policy.

Herd Replacement Policy

Herd size may well affect this decision. The larger producer may decide to run a closed herd multiplication unit to provide his own crossbred female replacements. This calls for the specialist skills of operating a specific breeding policy, following mating patterns and selection of suitable gilts to provide a regular flow of breeding stock for the main commercial herd. Some producers will prefer to buy in replacement gilts in a regular planned programme to fit in with overall mating targets and to maintain herd size. Buying in gilts is the first choice of many large-scale producers. This allows them to concentrate on the job of commercial production, while the breeding company supplies the long-term genetic improvement.

Maiden or Weaner Gilts

Where a producer is buying in replacement gilts there is a choice between maiden gilts, which will be about 95 to 105 kg liveweight at delivery, or weaner gilts at about 30 kg liveweight. Selected maiden gilts can quickly be integrated into the main herd after acclimatisation and in most cases will be sound and guaranteed to breed. Buying in weaner gilts provides a longer acclimatisation period, which may be helpful if there is a specific herd health problem. Special accommodation such as straw yards may be required for a short period to bring the weaner gilts up to a suitable age and weight for first mating, and there will be a need for some screening and selection at this point. Acclimatisation procedures will be discussed in the chapter on health.

Breeds and Lines

Females For homebred replacements the female line will almost certainly be based on the Saddleback breed, using a Landrace boar to produce a first-cross blue female. The Saddleback breed contributes an adequate level of backfat cover for outdoor production, as well as imparting a strong maternal instinct in the blue mother. The Landrace, which is also prolific, makes a contribution through good growth characteristics as well as lowering backfat levels. The Hampshire breed has been used with some success as an alternative to the Saddleback in producing a first-cross blue female for outdoor production.

Market demands for improved grading, with lower fat levels in the carcases of the final progeny, are prompting breeders to investigate other breeds and crosses. The Duroc breed may be able to help in reducing fat levels whilst maintaining sufficient hardiness for outdoor production.

Bought-in replacement females will almost certainly be F_1 or three-breed crosses, which have been specially developed for the outdoor market, and which are part of a long-term continuous breed improvement system.

Males   Boars will almost certainly be purchased from breeding organisations, super nucleus herd members of the MLC Pig Improvement Scheme, or from reputable private breeders. They should, of course, be performance tested with emphasis on selection for feed efficiency and low backfat levels. The breed most widely used for crossing with the blue female is the Large White. This breed has a good reputation for working out of doors and is relatively docile when run in a group with other boars. The Large White boar used on a Saddleback × Landrace female will provide maximum hybrid vigour in the resulting progeny.

A number of breeding companies are now producing specialist sire lines and crossbred boars for use on the outdoor sows. Outdoor producers in future are likely to buy sire line parent boars which will perform well in an outdoor environment and produce the most profitable carcase for their particular market outlet.

Health

Outdoor herds have established an excellent track record for health standards. Records and surveys show markedly lower veterinary and medicine costs per pig produced than indoor production systems. Basic policy decisions that determine the health of the herd include:

Veterinary Supervision
Many outdoor herds follow a policy of using a veterinary consultant

Plate 2   Large White boar typical of many used in outdoor production to sire slaughter generation.

Plate 3   Saddleback sow with cross-bred litter in farrowing unit.

who specialises in outdoor pig production and who makes regular herd visits. This provides the professional expertise to set up and follow a disease prevention programme incorporating the latest veterinary knowledge and techniques.

Source of Breeding Stock
Most herds will be buying in males and females on a regular basis. Choice of the source of breeding stock replacements is a critical one, and will need consultation between the producer, his veterinary adviser and the veterinary consultant from the breeder or breeding organisation.

Vaccination Programme
This will be arranged in consultation with the veterinary adviser, according to the needs of the herd and the likely risk in the specific location. Routines for internal and external parasites will also be worked out similarly. Further details of health and the outdoor herd appear in Chapter Eight.

Feeding and Nutrition

Feeding the outdoor herd follows the principles of sow feeding that have emerged over the past few years. These place an emphasis on maintaining a fit but not over-fat sow during gestation, and feeding generously during lactation. Overall, this should help to prevent drastic changes in sow body weight, and avoid extremely thin sows at weaning and service. In the outdoor herd, where there is less individual sow treatment, this job is more difficult than in many indoor herds which are individually housed and fed. A slightly higher feed usage may be called for, as shown in recorded outdoor herds, than in recorded indoor herds.

Purchase of Feeds
Because of the physical form of the feed (large nuts or cobs) most outdoor herds will purchase compound feed rather than produce it at home on the farm. In most cases, one diet is fed during both gestation and lactation, and there is usually the opportunity to feed sows individually during the suckling period. At weaning, grading of sows into selected groups according to condition will allow more generous feeding levels for thinner sows.

Creep Feeding
As indicated earlier, most outdoor herds do not creep feed. At

weaning, young pigs appear to take readily to solid feed without any setback.

Management Systems, Recording and Staff

In most situations the outdoor producer has opted for weaning at three to four weeks of age. Most herds will also follow a policy of continuous weekly farrowing. This helps with boar utilisation, improves farrowing intervals, facilitates the handling of return services and is essential for maximising sow productivity.

Integration with the Arable Break

Outdoor pig herds on the arable farm have proved to be an excellent break in the arable rotation, with the breeding herd utilising the short-term grass leys. The grass break provides clean ground for the sow herd, as well as making a fertiliser contribution to the following crop. A typical rotation would be as follows:

1. Barley—undersown with ryegrass.
2. Hay or seeds followed by grazing (sheep or cattle).
3. Outdoor sows.
4. Wheat (winter).
5. Wheat.

Outdoor Herds on Rented Land

One interesting development is the arrangement of a contract system between an arable farmer and a pig farmer who is willing to operate on rented land during the break-crop period. This provides the landowner a profitable break in his cereal growing without the necessity to become involved in the complications of outdoor pig production. The tenant meanwhile, provided that he has reasonable long-term security, can establish an outdoor system with relatively little capital investment. The rent negotiated will reflect the type of land, the amount of land required, and local demand and supply. Current (December 1987) rents appear to be in the region of £250 per hectare.

Straw

Whether on owned or rented land, the outdoor herd will require a large amount of baled dry straw. Estimates are usually based on about one-quarter to one-third tonne per sow per year.

Staff

The key to the successful operation of an outdoor pig enterprise is undoubtedly the selection of suitable staff. They face a different range of conditions from those of their colleagues who work in indoor units. The outdoor pigman or woman needs different skills, and by preference has chosen the outdoor life. Many outdoor units operate with a three- or four-person team, so that each must be a team member, prepared to tackle a wide range of jobs, including maintenance and repairs to machines and equipment associated with outdoor pig-keeping.

With breeding stock spread over a large acreage the pigman needs to be physically fit, but above all should be good at the basic pig husbandry skills.

Large units working on a team basis provide a good opportunity for on-the-job training, so that promotion can be made from within the organisation.

As outdoor pig systems have become a recognised part of pig production, a number of young graduates are now coming forward from agricultural colleges and schools.

Identification and Recording

Identification by use of large plastic ear tags has already been referred to. They have improved recognition of breeding sows at critical times in the production cycle. Accurate record keeping, in less than ideal circumstances, is an essential job; information needs to be collected daily as events occur. In practice some form of diary or logbook for daily entries provides a practical approach. The data is then sent, at regular intervals, to a bureau or office for processing by computer. This is the method used by many established recording schemes such as the Meat and Livestock Commission *Pig Plan*, which has over forty outdoor herds on record. However, all depends on the accuracy and quality of data collected by the staff looking after and supervising the pig unit.

Marketing

Choice of Market Outlets

Correct marketing of the products of the outdoor herd is necessary for the financial success of the enterprise. Traditionally, many of the store pigs from the outdoor blue sow finished up with specialist feeders who fed domestic waste by-products, and who then channelled the pigs at slaughter weight into live auction or to the manufacturing trade. More recently, changes resulting from breed improvement programmes and careful choice of feeding methods have led to a situation where the slaughter generation will meet

Plate 4   Group of Duroc gilts.

grading standards for the pork and cutter markets. Hardiness in the sow requires a reasonable level of subcutaneous fat for insulation and energy reserves, which results in the progeny carrying too much backfat to meet the very stringent grading requirements for bacon pig production.

Finishing on Farm of Origin
A usual choice for finishing is to transfer the weaners to specialist weaning accommodation on the producer's own farm, followed by growing the pigs through to final slaughter weight as in a farrow-to-finish operation.

Selling Store Pigs
A long-established alternative is to house the weaners in specialist accommodation, and then move them into general-purpose buildings or strawyards. They are then sold, under a regular contract, as strong stores at about 30–50 kg liveweight.

Selling Weaners
A more recent development is to sell the weaners directly off the field at three to four weeks of age. This needs to be carefully organised, and should be done as a direct producer-to-producer arrangement, without co-mingling of pigs from various sources.

Movement and mixing of early-weaned pigs can lead to a health breakdown and disaster.

Financial Planning

It is already clear that many outdoor herds are recorded in a number of schemes. There is no exact count of the number of outdoor herds, but it may be assumed that a larger proportion of them have their physical and financial performance recorded than is the case with indoor herds. Recording of physical performance is an essential prerequisite to operating a pig enterprise as a business.

Many existing producers already operate with clearly set physical and financial targets which are monitored and reviewed regularly.

Any producer considering establishing a new outdoor unit, or existing producer contemplating a major expansion, should follow a prudent business approach and prepare detailed budgets and cash flows. Figures and estimates used should be realistic and appropriate to the specific circumstances. Sensitivities for major inputs and outputs should be established in order to make realistic projections.

Guidelines, which should be used with caution but which were correct at the time of writing, are given later in this book.

Summary of Basic Policy Decisions

A successful outdoor pig enterprise will depend on a combination of unusual ingredients. Some climatic factors, such as rainfall and winter temperatures may be outside immediate control, but the choice of suitable free-draining land is fundamental.

The outdoor pig unit properly belongs to the large arable farm, and must be an integral part of the arable rotation. To these factors must be added the essential husbandry skills and specialised management expertise if the system is to work efficiently.

Other facts, such as breeding stock, feed supply and health control, whilst in themselves important, are not so critical as climate, suitable soil conditions and experienced and dedicated staff.

Chapter Three

THE SYSTEM, HOUSING, FENCING AND EQUIPMENT

THE SYSTEM

Introduction

IT IS POSSIBLE to set out a general description of the principles of outdoor pig production, but there can be no specific blueprint. As with most livestock enterprises there are many variations, and circumstances will change with each farm situation and geographical location. Some of these variations and innovations will be discussed later in this book, but the general assumption made for this summary is that sows and boars will remain out of doors throughout the whole of their reproductive cycle.

Figure 3.1 sets out the production cycle in diagrammatic form.

The Arable Rotation

Outdoor pigs will normally use the grass break in an arable rotation, and will need to move on to new ground every one or two years. Sometimes the herd spends the winter on the stubble and moves back on to grass in spring to take advantage of spring grazing. The stubble is then ploughed for a spring cereal crop. A variation on this is to move the sows on to outdoor leys in September, towards the end of the first year of a two-year grass break. The sows would stay on the ground until late the following summer, when the grass would be ploughed for a winter cereal crop. Outdoor pigs are most frequently followed by wheat, sometimes by potatoes, which take advantage of the pig muck left on the ground.

Some producers move the herd twice a year, others will lay out new ground and move half the herd each year. Many combinations have been used to fit into the individual farm situation, provide clean ground for the pigs to move on to, take advantage of the manure, and minimise labour demand for fencing and resiting of huts, equipment and services. Long term, this use of pigs in the arable rotation may have beneficial effects on the soil structure, as well as reducing the need for use of artificial fertilisers.

Owned or Rented Ground

Most herds are owned and operated by the landowner, who may set up a separate livestock company which operates as a separate business and profit centre.

In recent years there has been a trend towards the establishment

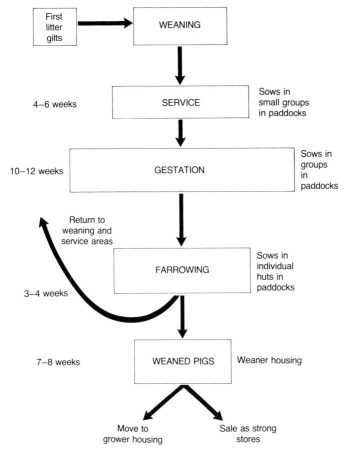

Figure 3.1   Typical production cycle for outdoor herds.

of 'nomadic' outdoor pig units. In this case a landowner rents out a suitable parcel of land to an outdoor producer on an annual tenancy. This method is most frequently used by a young, enthusiastic pig farmer, who can get into pig production with a comparatively small amount of capital outlay. The arrangement provides the landlord with a suitable break in the arable rotation without involvement in the specialist area of outdoor pig production.

Choice of Management System

Most outdoor units run the breeding herd out of doors as previously mentioned. Weaning takes place at three to four weeks of age, and the weaners are then moved to specialist buildings on the same farm. These progeny can be fattened on home mill-and-mix rations from cereals grown on the farm.

Land Requirements and Stocking Density

The amount of land required for an outdoor pig herd will depend on soil type, local climate, the shape and location of the land available, and age of weaning. Allowances must be made for roadways and access between paddocks. The general rule in practice seems to be about 14–19 sows per hectare overall. A 480–500 sow breeding herd will need a total of about 25–35 hectares.

The total land available will be subdivided by electric fencing into suitable sizes of paddocks. Stocking densities will vary at different stages during the reproductive cycle, and these will be discussed in a later chapter.

Integration with the Arable Farm

There are some other factors to consider, apart from the role of the outdoor herd in the arable rotation. These include the provision of the large amounts of straw that are needed all the year round. Some help may be needed from the arable staff for carting and stacking a year's supply of straw. At other times the pig team may need help with moving fences and equipment as the pigs are rotating between sites. Machinery and workshop facilities may also need to be shared for repair and maintenance of vehicles and equipment. Access to a portable welder or facilities for puncture repairs in the workshop can be a lifesaver at crucial times. This interchange of staff between arable and pig departments usually works well and helps to reduce peak demands in both enterprises.

Grassland Farms

In the south-western counties there have been a number of smaller outdoor herds set up on grassland farms. These are frequently operated by an owner-manager who has another livestock enterprise, such as dairying or sheep. Land and ground conditions are again critical, and use is sometimes made of wooded areas or scrubland. Grassland that has been used by pigs will be ploughed and reseeded for grassland improvement.

LAYOUT OF PADDOCKS

In practical terms, layout of paddocks will vary enormously according to the size of the herd, the soil type, topography and the amount of land available.

These layouts are given as examples of different plans used by commercial outdoor breeding herds, all weaning at three weeks of age, and working on an overall stocking density of between fourteen and nineteen sows per hectare.

1. 480–500-sow herd with an average of 20–22 farrowings per week

2. 100-sow unit with an average of five sows farrowing per week

3. A 60-sow module with regular farrowings, on average, of twelve sows per month

4. A radial paddock layout

480-Sow Requirements

Service Paddocks—Sows
At weaning, groups of ten sows are moved into service paddocks of about 0.6 hectare each, which also hold a group of four or five working boars. Four service paddocks are provided, which allows for the weaned sows from two weeks' weanings to be divided into four sub-groups. Sows can be sorted at weaning according to condition—'fats' and 'thins'. Feed levels can then be adjusted to meet the requirements of each group. Increased feed intake immediately after weaning will help to reduce the number of days from weaning to effective service. Sows are served in these paddocks, and remain in the same groups for up to four weeks, when two groups can be combined to make up numbers of 20–22 in the main gestation paddocks.

Gestation Paddocks—Sows
Each group of 20–22 sows in gestation will require a paddock of
about 1.2 hectares. For the first five or six weeks in the gestation
paddocks, one or two boars are run with the group to pick up
returns to service. A total of 16–18 gestation paddocks will be
needed. Total area for 'in-pig' paddocks for the 480-sow breeding
herd will be in the region of 19 to 22 hectares.

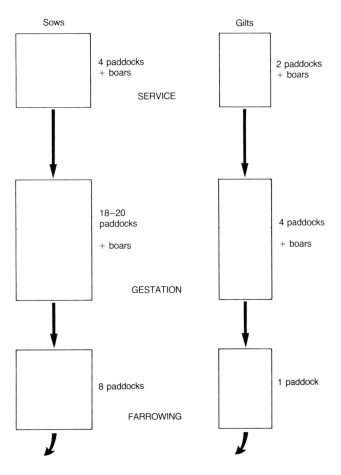

Figure 3.2   Pig flow through the paddocks, 480–500 sow outdoor unit.

Farrowing Paddocks—Sows
Each farrowing paddock will be about 0.6 hectare, and a total of eight will be required. A group of ten to twelve sows will be moved in one week before farrowing. Each paddock will contain ten to twelve farrowing huts, laid out in rows of five or six, the huts being spaced about twenty metres apart. Weaning takes place about the end of the third week of lactation, and newly weaned sows will be returned to the service paddocks. Weaners will be collected up and moved indoors.

Service and Gestation Paddocks—Gilts
A 480-sow unit will require fifteen or sixteen replacement maiden gilts per month to maintain herd size, and they will be delivered regularly each month. Six paddocks will be needed, each of 1.2 hectares. The first paddock is used for acclimatisation and also for training to the electric-fence system. The second is used for service, and will hold a group of boars of a suitable size. The remaining four paddocks are used by in-pig gilts and each group will run with a catch boar. Gilts are then moved to their farrowing paddock one week before due.

Farrowing Paddocks—Gilts
A separate farrowing paddock should be provided for gilts to reduce the risk of bullying by older sows. These gilts join the main breeding herd after the weaning of their first litters.

A total of nine farrowing paddocks will be required for sows and gilts, having a total area of 5.4 hectares.

Summary of Areas Required

	hectares	
Service	1.2	
Gestation	21.6	13.5 sows per hectare
Farrowing	5.4	(5.5 sows per acre)
Gilts	7.2	
Total	35.4	

Alternative Service Methods
There are many variations on this main pattern, and outdoor producers are always exploring different methods and trying out new ways to maximise production from their outdoor herds. Special attention is directed towards weaning and service areas. One

Plate 5 Group of Camborough Blues eating up their daily feed allowance in wintry conditions in Norfolk.

Plate 6 Sows outdoors in farrowing paddocks with tobacco barn in background. Kentucky, USA.

Plate 7   Group of Duroc cross White sows in outdoor conditions in Iowa, USA.

Plate 8   Landrace boars with Saddleback sows in service paddocks.

method is to use all the gestation paddocks in rotation for weaning and service of sows.

At weaning, sows and boars are placed in the next available empty paddock. Weaned sows can be sorted according to condition, and suitable groups made up, when weaning twice-weekly. It will be necessary to add an extra hut to the paddock to provide accommodation for the group of working boars. This hut can be moved on to another paddock when the main group of sows has been served. In this way, the group of sows stays in the same paddock from weaning until removed just before farrowing. Groups of boars and an extra hut are moved from paddock to paddock as required for groups of newly weaned sows.

One Hundred Sows—Three-week Weaning on a Weekly Basis

Service Paddocks
Groups of five sows, at weaning, are run with two boars, and four service paddocks are required. The boars run with the group to catch the 21-day return-to-service period. Paddock size will be approximately 0.3 hectare.

Gestation Paddocks

Two groups of sows are then combined to form groups of ten in the gestation paddocks. A total of six paddocks, each of 0.6 hectare, will be needed. A catch boar runs with the group to detect and serve any sows returning to service six weeks after first service. The final groups will be reduced to five sows when they are fourteen weeks in pig, and prior to moving to the farrowing paddocks.

Farrowing Paddocks

Five paddocks are needed, each of 0.3 hectare. Sows are in groups of five when moved into farrowing paddocks one full week before farrowing. Three weeks after farrowing, sows are weaned and moved back to the service paddocks. Gilts are slotted into the system as required to maintain herd size (see figure 3.3).

Summary of Ground Area Required

	hectares	
Service	1.2	
Gestation	3.6	14 sows per hectare
Farrowing	1.5	(5–6 sows per acre)
Service area		
and access	0.7	
Total	7.0	

Sixty-Sow Module, Weaning at Three Weeks and Farrowing Monthly

Multiples of the sixty-sow modules can be used to build up the required herd size. The module is based on sows farrowing, weaning and being mated each week.

Service and Gestation

A total of five dry sow paddocks is required, each holding twelve sows. The paddock holding newly-weaned sows carries three boars, and the next two paddocks each hold catch boars to pick up sows returning to service. Females remain in the same paddocks and are only moved at point of farrowing. Boars are moved around the dry-sow paddock system, reducing the need for movement of sows.

Farrowing Paddocks

Four farrowing paddocks are needed, each containing three farrowing huts, and every week three sows are moved into one of these

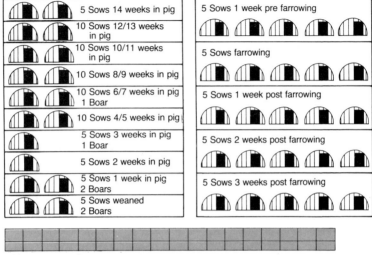

18 Weaner Units Containing 405 pigs.

Figure 3.3   Pig flow through a 100 sow unit.

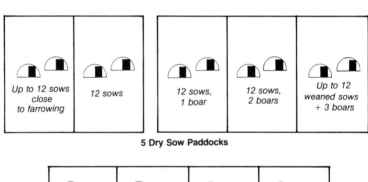

5 Dry Sow Paddocks

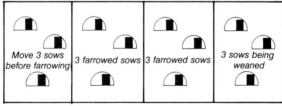

4 Farrowing Paddocks

Figure 3.4   Pig flow through a 60 sow unit.

paddocks. They are filled in rotation, and weaning takes place at three weeks of age. After weaning, sows are accumulated over a four-week period back in the first service paddock (see figure 3.4).

Radial Paddock Layout

A striking alternative to the traditional paddock layout has been developed by farmer/consultant Alec Jones, on his Oxfordshire farm, for his 240-sow outdoor herd. He developed the system over four years ago, based on a radial pattern.

All the paddocks are laid out within a large circle on an open and relatively level site without hedges, ditches or other obstructions. With a stocking rate of 15–16 sows to the hectare, the total area required for 240 sows is between 14 and 16.6 hectares. The herd is moved to a similar alternative site every two years as part of the arable rotation.

There is a small service area at the centre or 'hub' of the circle, from which most sow and weaner movement is carried out. Long, narrow working paddocks radiate out in a pie-shaped wedge pattern, from the centre to the perimeter fence. Separate access trackways are left from the main entrances to the central service area. A wide circular track follows the perimeter fence to give access to each paddock for feeding and servicing of water points. (See figure 3.5.)

All pig movement is effected through the central hub, and boars, sows and gilts can be moved quickly and easily with the help of gates and hurdles. At weaning, sows are driven to a vacant mating paddock and weaners into a special catching area, then into the livestock trailer.

The central service area holds a small container building which is used as an office, equipment store and changing room. There are also handling facilities for ringing and treating adult breeding stock.

This layout allows one man, with some part-time help, to manage up to 250 sows. Pig movement and handling are simplified, and the compact layout affords easy observation and control of the whole system.

SERVICE TRACKS AND ACCESS AREAS

Whatever the herd size, any layout needs to provide good access for vehicles and machinery.

Outdoor pig production involves a large amount of animal and vehicle movement, so areas of at least ten to twenty metres width

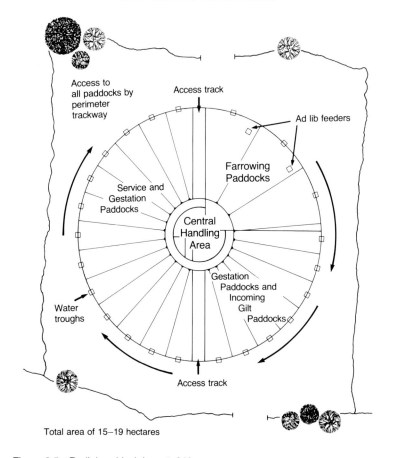

Total area of 15–19 hectares

Figure 3.5　Radial paddock layout, 240 sows.

should be left between rows of paddocks to provide sufficient turning room for vehicles.

Sufficient room should be allowed to give tractors plenty of track space to prevent wear and tear being caused by running on the same strip of land, which will eventually damage soil structure. Field boundaries and permanent fences will often dictate access routes, but careful planning will save both time and vehicle fuel. Tracks that appear easy in summer can be impassable in winter, especially if steep slopes are to be used as main access routes.

HOUSING, FENCING AND EQUIPMENT

Introduction

Layout and paddock size will vary from farm to farm because of herd size, land type and availability, and a number of other factors. Most outdoor pig producers use a similar and fairly narrow range of housing and equipment. Some equipment manufacturers have been in business for thirty to forty years, making well-designed and farm-tested products.

In recent years, new manufacturers have entered the market, especially in the area of fencing, handling and movement of outdoor pigs.

Pig Housing

Farrowing Huts

The traditional design has remained largely unchanged over the years. Huts are timber-framed, half-round structures, clad on the roof with curved sheets of 22-gauge galvanised corrugated iron. The huts are fitted with wooden backs and half-open fronts to provide access. Huts are not supplied with floors because deep straw bedding is used during the farrowing period. The straw is held inside the hut by a retaining board. To keep the litter confined, a special weaner run, sometimes called a fender, is fitted. The inward angled sides prevent the litter getting out, but the sow is able to step over and has freedom to come and go as she pleases.

In recent years fully insulated huts have become available, which help keep the sow and litter warmer in winter and cooler in summer. Doors can be provided to shut the pigs in if necessary, and hooks and brackets are usually fitted to help with handling and movement of huts.

Variations in design include steel backs and half-fronts rather than timber, and height, length and breadth measurements may vary slightly. Most huts used to be supplied ready made, but now more often come in a kit form which can easily be assembled on the farm. Whatever the design, huts should be well sealed and draught-free.

A recent newcomer to the farrowing hut range is the Pigloo which is made of glass-reinforced plastic. Similar in size and function to the wooden huts, the Pigloo is light and easy to move, requires little maintenance, and is rust-free. The thermal properties of the glass-reinforced plastic provide very good insulation, and a fender can be fitted.

The Pigloo has now been in use for over five years and is used on a number of farms in various parts of the country.

Typical Specifications of Wooden Huts

Sizes	1400 × 2500 × 1000 mm high
	1500 × 2500 × 1000 mm high
Weaner Runs	1300 × 1300 × 340 mm high

Dry-Sow Huts
Similar in construction and materials to the farrowing hut, the dry-sow hut has a rather simpler function to perform. Groups of sows and boars in the gestation paddocks are generally stocked at a rate of five or six animals per hut. In some cases this can be as high as ten to twelve per hut, depending on the size of the hut. A dry-sow hut measuring 2.5 m × 2.5 m would typically house four to six sows. An alternative design—still half-round in shape—uses plywood and a solid wooden floor, with skids for easier movement. The extra cost of the wooden floor may be justified if straw is in short supply, but generous use of straw is an integral part of the outdoor system, and performance may be affected if a plentiful supply is not available. Dry-sow huts need more maintenance than farrowing huts because of group occupation and housing of boars. Huts are supplied in kit form, with a selection of size adjustments in multiples of 750 mm.

Fencing

Introduction
The traditional fencing methods for outdoor pigs relied on wooden posts, pig netting and barbed wire, and wooden hurdles. All this has been replaced by the electric fence, which has been one of the factors responsible for the growth in popularity of the system. Electric fencing is cheaper, more versatile, and can be moved more easily than the older fences.

Electric Fencing
The system can operate from mains or battery. The best way is from mains high-voltage supply, but high-voltage tractor battery units are available. The high-voltage system gives a good 'kick' when touched and is now in use for a wide range of farm animals including dairy cattle, sheep and horses. Equipment which provides adjustable voltage levels is advantageous.

The most common system uses two strands of wire (16 gauge) attached by insulators to 10 mm mild steel posts. These posts are usually 1 metre long, with a 150 mm steel crosspiece welded 200 mm from the bottom. Most insulators allow for adjustment, to take account of changes in ground contours. The fence posts should be eight to ten metres apart, depending on ground conditions and contours. The wires should be set about 200 mm and 500 mm above ground level, which should be adequate for most needs.

Some producers use three strands in farrowing and gilt paddocks. These should be 100 mm, 250 mm and 530 mm above ground level.

When setting up paddocks, it may be helpful to use a weedkiller to kill a strip of vegetation immediately below and on the line of the wire.

A number of different types of wire have come on to the market to replace the standard soft wire. These include multi-strand polythene wire and a new wire which combines vinyl-coated glass fibre and aluminium alloy. This multi-strand 'Hotwire' is lightweight and easy to work with, and it offers conductivity up to twenty times that of stainless steel and polythene wire. Other developments include woven high-visibility fence tape, and alternative lightweight materials for fencing stakes and insulators.

Plate 9 Radial lay-out showing part of central race with access to gestation paddocks.

A wooden stake is still the best choice for corner posts for straining, using a piece of alkathene pipe as an insulator to take the wire around the corners.

Finally, a good earth connection is essential. This has sometimes proved difficult on dry sandy sites, and the only answer seems to be—dig deeper! For battery-operated units, security can sometimes be a problem, and batteries should be well secured—or booby-trapped!

Gateways and paddock entrances can be fitted with electrified gates made from coiled retractable wire, fitted with a special hand-piece which allows the operator, safely and quickly, to make a gateway through the electrified fence for access. Plastic wire netting used for sheep fencing is expensive compared with two strands of wire, and has been found to be not very practical when used for outdoor pigs.

Training paddocks for gilts are best laid out with a double strand of wire set up a couple of metres inside a visible standard pig-netting fence. A few shocks quickly train gilts to respect the system and stay within the boundaries of the electric fence.

Vehicles

Movement of Pigs

There are large numbers of livestock movements on the outdoor unit, and the need for ample turning and operating room between paddocks has already been mentioned. Most outdoor units use a livestock trailer to move stock, as moving sows by walking can be tedious, time-consuming and frustrating. Most sows are unwilling to cross fence lines, so a livestock trailer that can be driven to the boundary or into the paddock is the usual choice. Ideally, all the pigs in the paddock should be moved in one load, which saves a lot of chasing. A low loader with flotation tyres, tandem axles and a wide, spring-loaded tailgate is useful. Sides should be at least 1.2 m high, but some livestock trailers are fully enclosed. A side door will help with the loading and handling of the three-week-old weaner pigs. The trailer can also be used as a 'pig-handling centre' with the addition of hurdles and a crate with a headgate for eartagging or ringing.

There are a number of commercial livestock trailers on the market specifically designed for the outdoor producer. Two trailers may be needed for a 480-sow unit.

A livestock box attached to the three-point linkage of the tractor can also be used for fetching and carrying odd items of equipment, single boars, cull sows, casualties and carcases.

Feed and Straw
A trailer will be needed for daily feeding and for moving straw, although straw may be handled on foreloaders or with special handling equipment for big bales.

Tractors, Equipment and Staff
Tractors will obviously be needed to haul feed and livestock trailers, although a Land Rover could be used for the job. One of the tractors should be fitted with a foreloader and a rear-linkage transport box as already described. This will also be used for moving and handling huts and fencing, as paddocks are relocated.

Last but not least, some form of staff transport is essential. This could be a Land Rover, pick-up, or similar vehicle, but four-wheel drive should be considered essential.

A recent arrival on this scene is the rough-terrain vehicle. This three- or four-wheeled lightweight machine with low ground pressure tyres can keep going in the stickiest of conditions. Electric starting and good manoeuvrability make them handy for getting around the farm, as a personnel carrier or for pulling a trailer—and it is fun to drive anyway!

Other Facilities and Storage

If straw storage is not available in the main farm building complex, it may be necessary to store straw in stacks outside. Keeping straw dry and free from vermin becomes a major problem. Central bulk storage is also needed for feed, which will be collected from the central point for daily distribution around the paddocks.

A central office will be needed for recording, telephone, messages and storage of veterinary requirements and medicines, along with small items of equipment and tools. If the paddocks are a long way from the main buildings, a small portable building may be needed; a secondhand caravan, or a modified container box will often do the job of providing shelter, storage area, wash and brush-up and toilet facilities.

From time to time some emergency will arise, and it will be necessary to catch and restrain a sow or boar. Some strong wooden hurdles, stacked in a strategic place, should do the job together with some means of fixing the hurdles together to be secure enough to resist a wild boar!

Water Supply and Equipment

A regular water supply for the outdoor herd is essential. For a 480-sow unit, in summer, daily usage could be as high as 11,000–13,500 litres for drinking. With spillage and wallows this could add up to 23,000 litres a day.

Black alkathene pipe, 12.5 or 19 mm, is the universal choice, and is frequently mole-ploughed in to a depth of 300 mm below ground. This will mostly—but not always—solve the problem of freezing up in winter. Spurs to water points from the main alkathene supply pipe can be laid above ground, and these may be the only sections that need to be thawed out in frosty weather. Some producers prefer to keep all pipework above ground for better visibility and fewer problems in thawing out.

Drinking troughs, holding about 250–350 litres of water, are made of heavy-duty galvanised sheeting or cast iron, with a protected, pig-proof ball valve. Metal bars prevent the sows from lying in the trough. If pigs are weaned at three weeks the main concern is for sow drinkers, and conventional galvanised rectangular water troughs can be used. Pipes lying on the surface will not normally be attacked by breeding stock, providing that the system is functioning and there is an adequate water supply. Empty surface pipes can be dismantled very quickly by a few disgruntled breeding sows.

Freeze-ups in winter can still be a problem, as in the late second half of the 85/86 winter. In heavy frost thawing out the system may be out of the question, and a stand-by emergency system should be brought into action. The best answer is a wheeled water tanker (or bowser) holding 4,500 litres, pulled around the paddocks by tractor, or a flat-bed trailer carrying two 2,000-litre water tanks. Farrowing sows have the greatest need, but all water troughs will need some water every day until the thaw comes.

WEANER HOUSING

Pigs outdoors are weaned at three to four weeks of age into a variety of accommodation. This will vary from containerised flat-deck units to strawyards. Description will be confined to one type of housing, which is known as the weaner ark or weaner bungalow house. A variation on this is the Trobridge weaner house, developed by Geoff Wickens at Pig Breeders Supply Co., and widely used for early weaning of outdoor pigs.

Weaner Arks

Construction
Developed over thirty years ago by BOCM at Stoke Mandeville as an alternative to the outdoor straw bale shelter for early weaning, the ark is a free-standing unit which can be placed over slurry pits or on concrete slabs. A low-volume, solid-floor kennel is provided, with access through a pop hole to a slatted outdoor run. A door for the pop hole allows the pigs to be shut in the kennel or the run as required.

Feeding takes place inside the kennel, in feeders or on the floor, and a drinker is placed outside in the slatted area.

Ventilation is by an adjustable sliding panel in the back wall. The sliding lid of the kennel can be adjusted to provide extra ventilation, and successful management depends on setting the right stocking rate, with careful control of ventilation. Understocking in the initial stages may lead to pigs being cold and dunging inside the kennel. Training boards and pen dividers can help to overcome the problem, or the unit can be tightly stocked for the first two weeks, then the groups split down and moved into separate units.

Typical size of a unit to house thirty-six to forty weaners would be:

Covered kennel ark	2.4 m × 1.6 m
Outside run	2.4 m × 1.2 m
Overall size	2.4 m × 2.8 m

Lids and floors of units are now fully insulated and, with fitted floors, whole units can be mounted on skids if required. If the unit is on a permanent base it can be fitted with a heated floor. This is very useful for newly weaned pigs in winter, or for a few days at any time of the year. A wide range of materials is available for the floors of the outside runs, including concrete slats, weldmesh, woven wire or expanded metal.

Management
With good management, the weaner ark has provided serviceable weaner accommodation for the pig weaned at three to four weeks of age. It is not suitable for pigs weaned at an earlier age. There are no energy costs (unless underfloor heating is used), but it needs regular maintenance to prolong its working life.

Stocking rate should be worked out at 122 kg per sq. metre (25 lb per sq. ft) so that forty weaners can be held for a period of three to four weeks, until they are approximately six to seven weeks of age.

They are then split down into two groups of twenty, and can remain in the arks until they are about nine to ten weeks of age, at a weight of approximately 20.4–22.7 kg, when they can be sold, or transferred to grower buildings. There are a number of manufacturers who build and supply these units, and the reader should refer to the list of equipment suppliers and manufacturers at the end of the book.

Another option is to place these free-standing units under an existing roof to provide shelter from the weather, though this must be considered as more of a benefit for the stockmen than for the pigs. Feeding, service and management can then be carried out under cover.

The NAC Pig Unit at Stoneleigh, Warwickshire, has tried out a wide range of weaner housing, which can be seen by appointment at the Pig Demonstration Unit.

The Trobridge Weaner Unit

Construction
The Trobridge Weaner Unit provides accommodation for pigs weighing between 6 and 35 kg, in outdoor kennels and runs which join together to form a continuous range. The enclosed kennel has a monopitch roof measuring 2 m × 2.3 m incorporating a 1.2 m × 1.2 m hinged door for feeding and inspection of the pigs.

The external cladding is of plywood and the cladding of internal walls is compressed asbestos sheeting. The height of the kennel at the front is 1 m, sloping down to 0.6 m at the rear. A pop hole in the front wall provides access to an outside run with weldmesh floor.

Natural ventilation is made possible by a hinged flap on top of the front section. A heated floor can be fitted, and this is recommended for pigs weaned at three to four weeks of age. A hinged pair of doors give access to the full width of the kennel for cleaning out and power washing. The outside run is 2 m long by 2.3 m wide, with 75 mm × 19 mm × 6.3 mm welded steel mesh flooring on wooden frames. The kennel can be divided by an internal partition if required.

Management
In winter, with heated floors, the unit can be used for weaners at three to four weeks of age, straight off the field. Feeding can be done on the floor or in specially designed hoppers, with access through the door in the monopitch roof. Water is supplied through a

nipple drinker in the outside run. Careful control of the flaps and roof door will supply adequate natural ventilation. For pigs weaned at under six weeks, the standard kennel can be divided in half and, with the heated floor, provides a very good environment. Various stocking rates are possible, depending on the number and size of pigs weaned and their length of stay in the unit. The manufacturers recommend:

Stage 1.   From three to six weeks of age. 15 to 20 pigs in each half of a divided unit with heated floor.

Stage 2.   From six to nine weeks of age. 15 to 20 pigs in the full-size unit with heated floor, which is only used in very cold weather.

Stage 3.   Nine to twelve weeks of age. 15 to 20 pigs in a full-size unit without heated floor.

These units could be placed under an existing roof, or a raised roof covering the passage can be supplied as an extra with the unit.

These comparatively low-cost units provide good accommodation for the relatively hardy outdoor weaner, weaned at three to four weeks of age. Running costs are low, and the outdoor environment provides very good, healthy conditions, with some isolation between pens. Careful management of ventilation and feeding will give results comparable to those in fully controlled environment cages or flat decks.

Where containers or flat decks exist it is possible to use them, but there is no doubt in my mind that in setting up a new unit, or extending an existing one, the weaner ark or Trobridge Weaner unit is the best solution.

Chapter Four

FEEDING

INTRODUCTION

THE BASIC DECISIONS on feed and feeding policy have been outlined in Chapter Two. Feed is still the major cost of pig production, and correct choice of sow feeding policy and methods will have a major influence on overall profitability. Feeding the sow cannot be treated in isolation, but must be seen against the background of breeding policy, environment, health and management practices.

CURRENT RECOMMENDATIONS FOR INDOOR SOWS

In recent years an enormous amount of research has been directed towards finding the best way to feed the breeding sow for optimum results, and one fairly simple objective seems to have emerged. That is, to feed the sow so as to maintain adequate condition throughout both the gestation and the lactation periods of the reproductive cycle. Condition loss should be kept to a minimum during lactation, since this will reduce the need to feed large quantities during pregnancy. Maintaining sow body condition and measuring it in an objective manner are not easy jobs for the commercial producer. For herds in full confinement sows can be assessed by 'condition scoring', measurement of backfat, or by weighing. The last two methods are impractical in many farm situations, so condition scoring is widely used. A simple measurement, carried out regularly, gives a good indication of fat and energy reserves carried by the sow.

Using the ADAS method of condition scoring, sows that are either too thin or too fat can be avoided by changes in feed levels for individual animals as necessary. Both extremes of condition depress sow performance. In particular, sows that are too thin produce low numbers born and have poor milking ability. After weaning they have a long interval to mating, often return to service, and end up as cull sows. Over-fat sows often produce smaller than average litters and have more difficulties at farrowing. These extremes in condition can be avoided by following a careful feeding programme throughout the reproductive cycle.

Although a sow condition scoring system may be difficult for the outdoor producer to follow precisely, it is worth the effort because the principles of maintaining adequate sow body condition still apply.

SPECIAL CONSIDERATIONS IN FEEDING THE OUTDOOR SOW

In feeding the outdoor sow, the following factors must be taken into consideration:

Fat Reserves

These sows, because of their breed makeup, will usually carry an adequate supply of backfat, certainly more than the commercial hybrid sow. Care should be taken not to deplete this reserve by underfeeding, especially during lactation or in winter.

Group System

The outdoor sow will normally be part of a group system, especially during gestation, and may get individual attention only during lactation. Management techniques for minimising this problem will be discussed later in this chapter.

Outdoor Gilts

Replacement gilts, whether they are purchased as weaners or as maiden gilts, will need a separate feeding pattern specific to their needs.

Boars

Boars in outdoor systems present a special problem because they are usually fed alongside newly weaned sows which are receiving a generous daily feed allowance.

Compound Feeds

Most pig producers on arable farms will sell quality cereals off the farm and buy back compound feeds for the outdoor breeding herd. The need to provide a sow feed in a suitable physical form for use outside is a determining factor in this situation.

Grazing—Straw Intake

An allowance can be made in spring for the value of grazing, but this should not be overestimated. At best it could lead to a saving on feed of 0.25 to 0.5 kg per sow per day. More difficult to determine is the value of straw the sow eats. It probably has little nutritional value, but acts as a gut fill, may help the digestive processes and is probably of some value to a sow which is a shy feeder.

Arable Residues

In some areas, there may be the occasional seasonal arable crop available. This could be potatoes, fodder beet or carrots. By-products from canning and freezing can also be used, all of which will lead to marginal savings on feed and costs, but at the same time cause problems of handling and distribution as well as increasing health risks.

STORAGE, DISTRIBUTION AND FEEDING METHODS

Bulk or Bag?

Buying compound feed in bulk will lead to considerable savings in the feed bill, since the difference in price between bulk and bag can be as much as £8 to £9 per tonne. Some producers accept the higher cost for the convenience of 25 kg paper bags, which can act as a good method of measuring the amount in each paddock. This can be very useful in a start-up period (for the saving in labour and reduction of waste).

Sow feed delivered in bulk will be conveyed or blown into bulk bins on the farm by the feed merchant—no easy job with large cobs or rolls. Bins need to be in good condition or they may be blown apart.

Distribution

From the bulk bin the food will often be measured or weighed into sacks for distribution by trailer, transport box or Land Rover. Alternatives include a feed container fixed to the three-point linkage of the tractor, a box on a flat-bed trailer, or a specially designed feed truck. In all cases, feed is measured or weighed out at the point of delivery adjacent to the paddocks.

Feeding Methods

Sow feeding should be done as quickly as possible to help to avoid fighting and stress, and wear and tear on fencing by reducing potential breakouts. Bags which have been weighed and loaded in a specific order to fit in with the feeding route are definitely the best approach, as the speed and ease of delivery have a great calming effect both on the pigs and the staff.

Feeding will normally be done on the ground, with feed spread out in a long line. The rule of thumb for space is approximately 2 metres per sow. Alternatively, feed can be dumped in small heaps; so long as care is taken to allow more heaps than the number of sows in the group. Sows in farrowing paddocks can be given some individual attention at this time, unless ad-lib feeders are in use.

The case for and against ad-lib feeding of sows during lactation will be discussed later in the chapter. If the ground is wet or heavily poached, some producers use temporary troughs for sow feeding in the gestation paddocks. Ingenuity and improvisation lead to a wide range of materials being used, including sleepers, plastic guttering and conveyor belts.

FEEDING PATTERNS

From the general principles of modern sow feeding, and taking into account the specific requirements for the outdoor sow, we can begin to work out a feeding pattern. Factors that must be considered include:

Climatic Conditions

Extra feed may be needed in cold, wet periods.

Are Grazing or Stubble Available?

A small allowance could be made for good grass or plenty of pickings on the stubble.

Sow Condition

Are there some thin sows at weaning which need an increase in feed level?

Diet Specification

In most situations, a medium-energy diet of around 13.0 MJ/DE kg with a crude protein level of 16 per cent, bought from a compounder, will be the diet of choice. This specification has been used to draw up a herd feeding pattern in which the reproductive cycle has been divided into three phases:

1. Weaning to Re-mating.
2. Gestation.
3. Lactation.

1. *Weaning to Re-mating*
There is good scientific evidence in both the United Kingdom and the United States that high feed levels after weaning help to reduce the interval between weaning and first service.

Table 4.1   Effect of feeding level after weaning-to-oestrus period
in primiparous sows

| | Feed levels (kg) | | |
	1.8	*2.7*	*3.6*
Proportion mated within 42 days of weaning	67	75	100
Proportion farrowing	58	75	100
Interval weaning to first heat in days	22	12	9

Source: Brooks and Cole, 1972.
Note: Those not coming on heat within 42 days of weaning were slaughtered.

A feed level of 4.0 to 4.5 kg per sow per day is advised, and should be continued until a few days after first service. As previously indicated, boars in service paddocks will also receive these feed levels. If sows are split into groups at weaning, the higher feed levels could be continued until sow condition in the thinner group improves.

2. Feeding in Gestation
Feeding can be divided into three periods:

• *First three weeks after mating*   For sows in good condition, there is some controversy about feeding in this period. Some authorities advise that feeding high levels for the first two to three weeks of pregnancy can increase embryonic mortality. However the evidence is not clear and I prefer to feed thinner sows according to condition, even if this means higher levels for the first few weeks of gestation. Feed levels should be around 2.5 kg per day at this period.

• *Three weeks after mating until three weeks before farrowing*   Feed levels should be set according to the overall condition of the group, but should be about 3.0 kg per sow per day. Avoid overfeeding as this may cause a reduction in feed intake during lactation, as Table 4.2 shows.

Table 4.2   Interaction between feed intake in pregnancy and lactation

Pregnancy intake (kg)	1.6	1.8	2.0	2.2	2.4	2.6
Ad-lib intake in lactation (kg)	5.9	5.9	5.9	5.3	5.0	4.9

Source: Hazzledine, *Dalgety Pig News*, Winter 1985.

• *Last three weeks of gestation*   Feed levels should be increased to a level of 3.5 to 4.0 kg per day during the last weeks of pregnancy. This may, in some situations, increase birthweights, and so reduce pre-weaning mortality. If birthweights in the herd already average around 1.35 to 1.5 kg liveweight per pig, this feed increase may not be necessary.

3. Feeding in Lactation
The objective should be to increase feed intake gradually for the first four to six days after farrowing, up to appetite level by a week after farrowing. The aim is to reduce fat loss in the lactating sow, and to minimise loss of condition. Management skill is needed to build up to a high intake, but a level of 6.0 to 8.0 kg should be the target.

An alternative method is to provide an ad-lib feeder in the farrowing paddock and to allow the sow full-time access to the feeder during lactation. Careful siting of the feeder is needed but most sows find it quickly after farrowing. The feeder should be serviced daily with fresh feed, and both access and feed wastage need careful monitoring. Newly farrowed sows can be fed individually, near or in their huts, for the first few days after farrowing. A few days after all the group has farrowed, feeding can be switched to ad-lib feeders. This calls for careful management and control of the ad-lib feeders. They should be run down and emptied before weaning, so that they can be cleaned out, ready and waiting for the new group of sows in the farrowing paddock.

Ad-lib feeding in lactation may lead to increased feed usage for a period of two or three weeks but should result in sows in better condition at weaning and may lead to a lower feed requirement in the next gestation period.

This brings us to the acid test of the system, that is, the balance between total sow feed usage, sow condition and sow productivity, including the working life of the sow in the herd. It is difficult to give a hard and fast ruling about ad-lib feeding systems in lactation, as producers hold strong (and differing) views on the topic. The best way is to give the system a carefully controlled trial over a reasonable period of time, collect the results, analyse them, then make some logical decisions in the specific farm circumstances. (See figure 4.1)

Gilts

Maiden

When maiden gilts join the main herd four or five weeks before service, they should be fed on the same diet as the sows (13.0 MJ/DE kg) at about 2.2 to 2.4 kg per head per day. They can be stepped up to 3.5 kg per day from a few days before they are put in with the boar until a few days after service. The actual level will depend upon gilt condition, but an increase in feed level at this stage will have a 'flushing' effect, which should help conception rates and increase numbers born alive. Feed levels can be reduced a few days after mating to around 2.5 kg per day, again depending on condition, season and any grass available. This feed level can be maintained until the last three weeks of pregnancy, when feed should be stepped up to 3 to 4.0 kg/gilt per day.

Increasing feed levels at this stage, as with the sow, should help to produce heavier birthweights and reduce pre-weaning mortality in

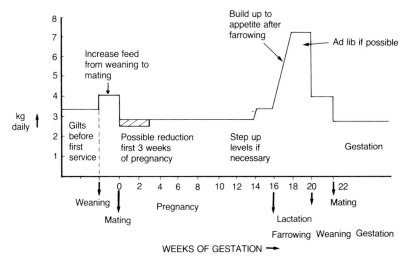

Figure 4.1 Suggested sow feeding profile.

gilt litters. Gilts should not be overfat at farrowing, and feeding gilts to get them fit but not fat is a good test of management skills.

Gilts during lactation should be built up cautiously to appetite level by the end of the first week after farrowing, or they can be fed ad-lib if that is the policy which has been selected. (See table 4.3.)

Careful assessment of gilts at weaning will give a very clear indication to the producer of the efficacy of the feeding programme that is being followed on the farm. Too many thin gilts will lead to delayed return to service and an overall reduction in herd reproductive performance.

Weaner Gilts
Weaner gilts will be delivered to the farm at about 30–35 kg liveweight. They should be fed ad-lib on a good quality grower type diet until they are about 80–90 kg liveweight. Increased levels of protein, minerals and vitamins in the grower diet will help with skeletal growth and development of the gilt in preparation for a working life out of doors.

At 90 kg liveweight, the gilt can be changed over to restricted feeding on the sow diet, at about 2.2 to 2.4 kg of cobs per gilt per day, depending on condition. The feeding pattern should then follow the programme as described for maiden gilts earlier in this chapter.

Plate 10   Farrowing paddocks in shelter of the wood.

Plate 11   Daily inspection of each individual farrowing hut is important part of daily routine.

Table 4.3 Summary of sow and gilt feeding patterns

Period	Daily intake (kg)
Sows	
Weaning to re-mating	4.0 to 4.5 kg
First three weeks after mating	2.5 to 3.0 kg
Three weeks after mating until three weeks before farrowing	3.0 kg
Last three weeks of gestation	3.5 to 4.2 kg
Lactation	First week build up to appetite, then ad-lib, or 7 to 8 kg
Gilts	
On delivery and during acclimatisation	2.2 to 2.4 kg
One week before and after mating	3.5 kg
Remainder of gestation	2.5 kg
Last two to three weeks of gestation	3.5 to 4.0 kg
Lactation	First week build up to appetite level, or ad-lib

Creep Feeding

As the sows are weaned at between three and four weeks, there is no need for creep feeding out of doors.

Feeding the Weaner

Introduction
Newly weaned pigs will be approximately three to four weeks of age, and housed in weaner bungalows or Trobridge type housing. Feeding really cannot be separated from the management of the pig, and reference should be made to the section in Chapter Five which discusses management of the weaner along with some performance guidelines and targets.

Diets
Pigs between three and four weeks will have an immature digestive system. They will not be able to deal easily with non-milk nutrients. Unabsorbed dietary components in the digestive tract may cause changes in the gut micro-flora, which may lead to some scouring in the first week after weaning.

A two-stage feeding programme is advised, with a starter type diet followed by a grower ration. The starter diet must be fresh and palatable, and should contain some milk products and cooked cereals. This starter diet can be fed from weaning until the young pig is ten to twelve kg liveweight, when a gradual changeover is made to the grower ration.

Initially the starter diet can be fed on the floor, and it may be better to underfeed rather than overfeed for the first few days. Feeding two or three times daily provides time for observation and stockmanship.

It is essential to prevent dehydration during the first few days after weaning, and cube drinkers placed in the weaner runs will help with this. The drinkers should be replenished with clean water daily. Special attention should be given to the group that contains the smallest and least thrifty weaners. Floor heating, or covering the outside run, will provide extra warmth, and a liquid milk supplement can be offered in the cube drinker for the first week after weaning.

From ten to twelve kg liveweight the weaners can be fed ad-lib on a grower diet, but feeders should be serviced daily to keep the feed fresh and to allow for observation.

Post-weaning diets should allow reasonable feed intakes, rapid growth, and good feed efficiency, with low mortality rates. All these factors are influenced by the environment, stocking rates and standard of stockmanship. Correct choice of feed and feeding methods immediately after weaning will have an important influence on the performance of the pig through to final slaughter weight.

Total Feed Amounts

Sows kept out of doors will use slightly more feed than sows housed in indoor systems. This is not surprising because of the need to feed more generously out of doors in winter, and the fact that outdoor systems are based on group feeding systems rather than on an individual basis as indoors.

The boars' share of feed intake will also be higher than in indoor situations because group feeding of boars outdoors is the only feeding method that can be used.

MLC recorded figures, along with Cambridge and Exeter survey reports, all confirm the slightly higher intake figure, which includes the boars' share of feed. A good target figure would be between 1.24 and 1.28 tonnes of feed per sow per year.

Chapter Five

MANAGEMENT

INTRODUCTION

THERE CAN BE no exact blueprint for management of the outdoor herd, but this chapter sets out some guidelines which are based on the practical experience of a number of successful large-scale producers. From a management point of view, compared with indoor production, the outdoor producer and his management team follow a much more individualistic approach. There appear to be more variations between outdoor producers than amongst those working with sows indoors, but the end result is more than satisfactory, whether measured in pigs produced per sow per year, job satisfaction or the operation of a successful business.

SOME ASSUMPTIONS

Some assumptions need to be made so that a number of management guidelines can be set out.

Location

Free draining site, light soil over chalk, central southern England on arable farm as part of rotation.

Herd Size

480–500 sows and 30–32 boars in commercial production.

Weaning

Weaning at three to four weeks of age with pigs moved to weaner arks directly off the field. No castration.

65

Replacements

All initial stock bought in as maiden gilts at 95 to 105 kg liveweight, with weaner gilts at 30–35 kg used for replacements thereafter. Boars bought in at 95–100 kg.

Staff

Three-man team including manager, responsible for all breeding herd activities including weaning and transfer of pigs off the field. (Farmer/owner.)

Health

All breeding stock bought from Nucleus and Multiplier herd within same breeding pyramid. Regular visits to herd by consultant veterinarian.

Finance

The assumption is also made that the necessary financial planning has been done, budgets and cash flows prepared and physical and financial targets agreed, and that the whole project is financially viable.

SETTING UP THE NEW HERD

Introduction

It is essential that the new unit should get off to a flying start and meet physical and financial targets which have been projected. In the early stages, careful monitoring and review of performance levels will be needed to keep the project on course.

Check List

1. Paddocks
- Laid out, prepared and fenced with power switched on.
- Training paddocks prepared for boars and gilts.
- Pathways, service and storage areas in position.

2. Breeding Stock
- Delivery pattern agreed on monthly basis, the first batch four to five weeks before first service date.
- Boars delivered ahead of gilts, with sufficient boar power for first few months.

3. Services and Supplies
- Water laid on and working.
- Suitable feed delivery organised.
- On start up it may be more convenient to take feed in bags. This will give a fresher supply of feed as breeding herd numbers build up, and better control of feed intake and overall feed usage. Switch to bulk supply later.
- Staff ready, trained and willing to go.
- Suitable recording programme worked out and operational from day one.
- Vehicles, equipment and communications all ready and working.
- Sufficient straw in storage.

MANAGEMENT OF BREEDING STOCK AT CRITICAL STAGES

The management of sows, boars and gilts at critical stages in the reproductive cycle will be described as follows:

Weaning
Weaning to service
In gestation
At farrowing
Gilts
Weaner gilts.

Weaning

Sows
A total of twenty to twenty-two sows will be weaned on a weekly basis. This can be done on one day, but is more likely to be twice a week, say Monday and Thursday. Sows would be sorted according to condition, with the fatter sows from two weanings going into one paddock and the two groups of thinner sows going into a separate paddock. Each paddock could hold ten to twelve sows and is then closed. A first group of boars would be placed in the paddock on the day of weaning, or might be held back and introduced twenty-four

or forty-eight hours later. They should be replaced by a second group several days later, according to work-load requirements.

The day before weaning feed levels can be slightly reduced. On the day of weaning, some producers move the livestock trailer to the centre of the paddock and feed half rations inside the trailer, so that the sows are already captured and ready to be moved. If transport is not used, then sows will have to be walked, enticed, driven and cajoled out of the farrowing paddocks and on to the service paddocks.

Sow performance will already have been reviewed and a number of sows will be culled. Target numbers of twenty-four to twenty-six for weekly mating will be made up by mating maiden gilts, although the gilts will be held in a separate system until after weaning their first litter. At this stage, weaned first litter gilts will graduate to the main herd and be introduced, with sows, into the service paddocks.

This is the appropriate stage to carry out recommended vaccinations, such as erysipelas, and treat for lice and mange if necessary.

Nose rings and identification should be checked, and ringing and re-tagging carried out as appropriate. Records should be brought up to date at this point.

Boars
Groups of three or four boars should be standing by and ready for work in the service paddocks. New groups of young boars may be coming up to work for the first time, and should be old enough and sufficiently large to do their job. Boars should be between seven and eight months of age and fully acclimatised before going out to work. Training may be necessary and their first mating may need supervision.

Mature boars, ideally, should never be mixed, but it can be necessary on some occasions because of culling or death. Boars should be de-tusked, matched for size if possible, and mixed with a group of sows that are on heat. Body odours should be masked with a manure wash or pig oil, and if necessary a mild sedative such as Stresnil should be used to help reduce the aggression. Stand by, however, for life saving removal of the odd boar that is taking a beating.

Weaners
Pigs should be collected, early in the morning when they are still in the farrowing ark, on the day of weaning. Some managers shut in the sow and litter the previous night, and in difficult cases the ark may have to be rolled over to catch the pigs. The usual method of

transport will be a livestock trailer and a side door in the trailer makes for easier handling. Hurdles and pursuit may be the only alternative if this technique fails.

A count is made and number weaned per sow recorded. Pigs are then transported off the field and transferred to the next stage of production, or moved off the farm for sale. With a total of twenty sows weaned, the weekly target will be in the region of 190–200 weaners transferred from the paddocks.

Weights should be in the range of 5 to 6 kg per weaner, but this will depend to some extent on litter size and exact age in days. Sizing and sorting of newly weaned pigs will be discussed in a later section in the chapter.

After weaning and removal of both sows and litters, the farrowing huts will be rolled over and the straw burnt on site. This straw burning, together with an 'all in – all out' system of managing the farrowing paddocks, is a good method of helping to control disease.

Weaning to Service

Sows
Group size, as indicated, will be no more than ten or twelve, which gives better control than is possible with very large groups at weaning. Sows should be fed at very generous levels between weaning and service, and comments have already been made about this in the chapter on feeding. The group of thinner sows should receive special attention, although it will mean that boars working with newly weaned sows will also be getting more feed than they actually require. This is unavoidable with an outdoor service system.

Most sows will come on heat within three to five days of weaning, but the odd one may need to be held over and mixed with the next week's weaning batch.

Boars
Outdoor sows may be served more than two or three times while they are on heat, often by different boars, but this is no great problem and in fact may be a positive advantage in terms of numbers born and farrowing index. Sufficient boars must be present in the service paddock, a ratio of three boars to ten sows is a good practical figure.

Each day sows that have been served should be marked and date of service recorded. If the boar is known, it is useful to make a note to help check his breeding performance. Services may be spread over a week, and this is the best time to check up on a boar's libido, work rate and general approach to his job. A boar that is lazy, lame, overweight or too aggressive may be a candidate for early replacement. Managers in most outdoor herds will let the boars get on with the job of mating. Husbandry and supervision of services is not carried out as it would be in an indoor herd, which depends on carefully controlled individual matings with boars kept separately from the newly weaned sows.

Successful mating and conception is a vital part of the outdoor sow system and survey records show farrowing rates well up to indoor standards. Some outdoor herds, however, have chosen to wean and serve sows indoors; these and other variations will be discussed in Chapter 10.

To summarise:
- Introduce groups of boars to newly weaned sows. If this is done at weaning it may help to reduce the fighting that is likely to take place.
- Sort out sows in groups according to condition.
- Feed sows generously between weaning and first service.
- Good observation, some detective work, and recording will help to keep results on target.

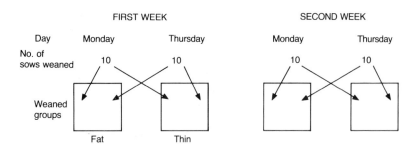

Figure 5.1   The twice-weekly weaning system.

Gestation

Sows

Sows that have been mated will stay in their service paddocks for three or four weeks. Feed levels for the sows in better condition can be reduced a few days after mating. Feed levels for thinner sows should be kept up, to improve their condition. At the end of this period, sows can be sorted back into groups of twenty to twenty-two, and be moved back into the main gestation paddocks where they will stay throughout the remainder of the pregnancy. Most of the boars can be moved back to work with other newly weaned groups of sows, but one or two will run with groups of sows for up to six or seven weeks after service to allow for any returns to service at three or six weeks.

Three or four gestation huts will be positioned fairly centrally in the paddock. They may need to be re-sited from time to time. Huts should be bedded up fairly generously with straw at least once a week. The exact amount will depend on the time of the year, with more generous amounts in winter.

If good handling facilities are available, pregnancy checking can be carried out, by machine, six weeks after first service, but it is more likely that pregnancy checking will be based on catch boars running with sows during the first part of pregnancy, and then by visual observation. Sows that look suspiciously empty become prime candidates for the pregnancy testing machine, and can be confirmed barren and then culled. Non-working boars and empty sows will need to be culled, and a special watch kept on the rest for signs of lameness which may need treatment with a long acting antibiotic. Sows that lose rings will need to be caught and re-ringed and a general eye should be kept on overall sow condition. Adjustments of feed levels may be needed according to the condition of sows in the group, climatic conditions and availability of grazing.

In summer, wallows should be provided to keep breeding stock cool, although in many situations these will be made by the sows themselves around watering points. A coating of mud will help prevent sunburn and, in rubbing off the mud, the sow may get rid of lice. As natural shade is only very rarely available, some producers provide shade. This can be done with camouflage nets or plastic netting (such as Netlon) suspended between bales or in a tent-like arrangement with upright wooden poles. Extremely hot weather can lead to infertility, and both sows and boars may be affected. Keeping both boars and sows cool with the help of wallows and shade will help to overcome what is sometimes referred to as summer infertility.

Feed levels, as suggested earlier, can be increased in the last two to three weeks of pregnancy, which may help increase litter birth weights. Sows due to farrow will be removed from gestation paddocks five to seven days before they farrow. They will need to be selected by eye, as not all service dates will be known precisely, and some sows will have to be moved back if they do not farrow with their own group.

It may be necessary in spring and early summer to top the grass with a forage harvester. This encourages re-growth of the grass sward and helps to control weeds.

Farrowing

The first priority is to make sure the farrowing paddocks are ready to receive the sows. The gestation groups will be divided again, back into two sub-groups of ten each. A few days should be allowed to let the sows settle down and become familiar with their new surroundings. Farrowing paddocks are usually laid out in a specific rectangular pattern, allocating one hut per sow, with the backs of the huts into the prevailing wind to prevent wind and weather getting through the sheltered doorway. Some producers cover the door opening with heavy-duty plastic strips. This allows access by sow and stockman, and improves the internal environment of the hut.

Rows of huts are usually placed 20 to 22 metres apart with 12 to 15 metres between huts. This provides each sow with her own territory around her own hut, and gives her reasonably good access to a central water point. Feeding can be adjacent to each hut if sows are fed individually, otherwise they will need to head for the ad-lib feeder.

Outdoor sows have freedom to build their nests before farrowing and lots of clean dry straw should be available. Chopped straw should be used when the hut is first bedded up to allow the sow to build a neat, compact nest. Newly born pigs are less likely to get tangled up in the short straw than in the conventional longer material. Topping up the hut afterwards can be done with normal length straw. Nesting behaviour and milk appearing in the teats is a sure sign that farrowing is imminent.

Most farrowings take place overnight, without supervision, although many producers will make a late night check of each farrowing group. Litters born overnight will be checked next morning, teeth clipped, tails docked and an iron injection given at the same time or on the following morning. Numbers and dates will be recorded in the daily diary, and the sow encouraged to take her first feed after farrowing.

All the sows in the paddocks should farrow within three to four days of each other, which allows for cross-fostering and matching up of litters. Intervention or aid for the sow farrowing outdoors is only rarely necessary.

Sows will occasionally double up, so one sow and half the piglets will have to be removed to an empty hut, and may need shutting in for twelve to twenty-four hours. In the first few days after farrowing, sow feed levels need to be built up to appetite level as quickly as possible. If an ad-lib feeder is provided, a close watch should be kept to see that all the sows are using the feeder regularly.

Litters need to be looked at daily inside the farrowing hut, as at farrowing the wooden or metal fender will have been placed in position at the door to keep in the young pigs. Topping up with straw two or three times a week will be necessary, and a daily count should be made, removing any dead pigs there may be. Removal of dead pigs and afterbirth helps to discourage visits by birds, vermin and foxes. Sows will forage around the farrowing paddock looking for grass, food and water but will return to their own huts for regular suckling, a pattern which should continue through to weaning. At weaning, huts will be rolled over and moved a few metres, straw and contents burnt as indicated earlier, and the huts made ready to receive the next group.

Gilts

Maiden Gilts

As mentioned earlier, selected maiden gilts should be delivered four to five weeks before required for service. They should be acclimatised, and trained for use with the electric fence. This is done by running a two-strand electric fence inside a conventional pig netting fence. If they break through the electric fence, they are at least contained within the main paddock fence.

They should also be ringed as soon as possible after arrival and be trained to eat sows' cobs or nuts fed daily in their paddocks. Ear tagging may also be done at this stage if required. Feeding patterns, as indicated earlier, should produce a gilt ready for mating at about 115 kg to 125 kg liveweight, at between seven to eight months of age.

Gilts at Service and Gestation

Gilts will be kept in separate paddocks from the main breeding herd, but feeding and management patterns are similar to those of the main herd. Groups of boars will need to be matched for size so that they are not too heavy for the maiden gilts. Vasectomised boars are frequently run with gilts to help stimulate heat and so that a pattern of oestrus can be more readily observed. The vasectomised boar will be removed before mating begins. Gilts need to be in good

Plate 12   Chopped straw is blown into farrowing hut to provide a suitable base for sows about to farrow.

Plate 13   Farrowing hut and fender.

condition at mating, after which feed levels will depend on season and any grazing that may be available. An active catch boar will run with the gilt group for seven to eight weeks after first service to cope with any returns to service. Pregnancy detection will be done by visual observations, with only the doubtfuls tested by machine. Condition should be maintained as the gilts approach farrowing, but they should not be overfat.

Gilts at Farrowing
Gilts need to be moved into their farrowing paddock at least a week before they are due, so they can settle down and, hopefully, select a farrowing hut each, rather than all piling into one hut.

More problems can be anticipated with farrowing gilts than with sows. There will be more doubles and triples in farrowing huts, more abandoned litters, and occasional savaging. These problems can mostly be dealt with as they come along, relying on the in-built docility and mothering instinct which should be an integral part of the temperament of the outdoor sow. Firm, quick action in moving gilts and their new litters to empty huts will sort out the situation and help the gilt group to settle down to a regular suckling pattern. A gilt sometimes needs to be shut in with her litter for twenty-four hours while she settles down, and it is useful to have a few plywood doors handy for this purpose.

Careful feeding, on the lines indicated earlier, building up to appetite levels a week after farrowing and preventing too much loss of body condition, will give the best results. Gilt litters may be slightly smaller at weaning than those of mature sows, and cannot be expected to match older sows' litters in number of pigs weaned. After weaning her first litter, the gilt will join the main breeding herd in the service paddocks to begin her next reproductive cycle.

Weaner Gilts

Many outdoor producers buy weaner gilts at around 30–35 kg live-weight because they find it easier to introduce and integrate them into the main herd by giving them a longer acclimatisation period on the farm than is possible with selected maiden gilts.

From delivery, weaner gilts should be fed ad-lib on a good quality grower diet as described earlier in the chapter on feeding. Many producers have straw yards available, which are ideal for hardening off weaners before they are put into the outdoor paddocks at 60 kg liveweight. Producers without yard accommodation put their weaner

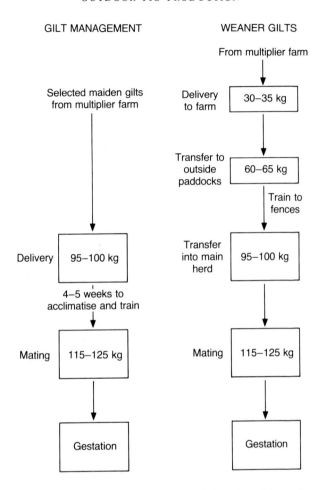

Figure 5.2 Management and feeding recommendations for maiden and weaner gilts.

gilts directly out of doors into paddocks adjacent to the main breeding herd.

When the gilts reach 60–65 kg liveweight, they can be moved into paddocks as suggested. These can also act as training paddocks to get them used to the electric fencing system. At the same time, they follow the farm acclimatisation procedures and can be changed over gradually to be on a restricted diet by the time they reach 90–95 kg liveweight.

At this stage they should be screened and selected in preparation for mating and joining the main breeding herd. Normal selection rate would be 80–85 per cent of weaner gilts bought, with unselected gilts rejected because of size (small pigs), poor conformation, indifferent legs or insufficient teats. Some producers will mate all weaner gilts purchased and cull after the first litter, but the earlier selection procedure is recommended. Selected gilts are then moved into the gilt service paddocks and the feeding and management methods set out for the purchased maiden gilts should be followed. Figure 5.2 summarises the management and feeding recommendations for both maiden and weaner gilts.

Boars

Introduction
Boars working on outdoor units require slightly different treatment than boars working under intensive conditions. In most outdoor units they will be working in small groups, and it is a good idea to have the group mixed together before delivery. Orders for new boars should be placed well ahead of the date they will be needed to begin work. This will allow the breeding company or breeder to mix the boars together when they come off test. Mixing with resident boars on the farm after delivery is not advisable, and may lead to injury or even death.

On Delivery
Allow some time for young boars to recover from the stress of transportation. Provide warm, dry clean accommodation with a good supply of water. If they are placed in an outside paddock, shade must be provided to prevent sunburn and sunstroke. Do not, at this stage, mix them with other breeding stock on the farm, as incoming stock should go through a period of at least three weeks acclimatisation. Resist the temptation to make a snap judgement of their merit by visual assessment; remember you cannot see the genetics. Better to wait until you can measure the performance of their progeny.

Acclimatisation
Allow a period of three to four weeks away from immediate contact with other pigs on the farm. This is the time to catch up with vaccinations, in line with the herd programme. Specific notes on

acclimatisation of breeding stock are set out in Chapter Eight (Health Considerations) later in this book.

Training
Acclimatisation should be followed by a vital period of training. Most boars will do what comes naturally, but this is not always the case, so that a period of boar training is advisable. By this stage, boars will be about seven to eight months of age, and training should be supervised by an experienced stockman.

Essential Rules
- After acclimatisation, pen young boars within sight and sound of sows on heat or adjacent to other boars at work.
- Observe and supervise the first few services. Provide small sows and gilts that are fully on heat.
- Provide good facilities for first services, with adequate space and a good non-slip surface if possible.
- Make sure vaginal entry takes place; some manual assistance may be necessary. Discourage boars from mounting the front end of the sow.
- If at first the boar does not work, do not persist. Try later in the day, or next morning. Young boars quickly become frustrated and exhausted.
- Do not allow bullying and savaging by sows or older boars to take place. Watch the boar/sow ratio with young boars. It may be necessary to remove a young boar from active service for a few days if he has been placed in a pen with too many sows to be served.
- Avoid excessive noise and rough handling during this training stage.

Problems
Most problems arise through failure to acclimatise correctly. Lameness and injury to the penis and testicles can put a boar out of action. Veterinary treatment may be necessary, but a few days rest will often restore the boar to working order. Over-use may lead to temporary infertility and, as made clear earlier, this should be avoided.

Careful handling and training of young boars pays off.

A well-trained boar will work unsupervised for the rest of his working life in a herd, with only the occasional check up.

MANAGEMENT OF THE WEANER

Management

The weaner produced outdoors seems to present fewer management and feeding problems than the same age pig reared indoors. The outdoor weaner is probably healthier, with fewer respiratory and intestinal problems than the weaner reared indoors.

It can be expected to weigh 5–6 kg, and a target figure for the herd with twenty litters weaned in a week would be 190 to 200 pigs brought in from the paddocks. On some farms these pigs may continue under the management of the outdoor staff, especially if they are being sold as stores. In other situations, if pigs are being grown on to full slaughter weight, there will be a change of staff and management.

In either case, the weaners will be sorted by sex and size. Boars and gilts will be penned separately, and there may be a mixed group of smaller pigs which will need special care; a heated floor or suspended heaters may come in handy, especially in winter.

Stocking rates will need careful planning according to space and type of housing available, but weaner arks are the likely choice. The arks that are to be occupied should have been power washed, cleaned up, and dried out in readiness, and an 'all-in-all-out' system should be followed. Thirty to forty pigs will be placed in one ark to conserve body heat and comfort, but will be later split into two groups of fifteen to twenty. (Reference to stocking rates is made in the section on housing the weaner pig in Chapter Three.)

Feeding will probably initially take place on the floor, and intake should be built up to ad-lib as quickly as possible. It may be necessary to feed five or six times daily for the first days, with a good quality starter diet. Clean drinking water is essential and it may be advisable to adjust the nipple-type drinker so that it provides a steady drip for the first few days.

After the weaners reach ad-lib feed levels, they can gradually be switched to a home-mixed cereal diet until transfer at 30–35 kg or point of sale.

Daily checking of piglet comfort is essential, with special attention to floor draughts, ventilation rates, lying room and access to feed and water.

Post Weaning Guidelines and Targets

The assumption is made that the weaner is 5 to 6 kg liveweight at three to four weeks of age. The following guidelines can be used as targets, but performance will be affected by the quality of the diet, critical temperature, stocking rates and disease status.

Temperature at Floor Level

At weaning	29°C
At 7 weeks	24°C
At 10 weeks	22°C

Growth Rates

- *Weights at various stages*

Weeks	kg
3 to 4	5–6
5	7–8
6	12–15
8	20–22
10	24–26
12	30–32

- *Overall growth rate*   A good target between weaning at three to four weeks, and twelve weeks of age, is an average of between 440–480 grammes per day.

Mortality
The target to aim for is a figure of between 1½ to 2 per cent at the most.

Feed and Water
- *Feed hopper space*, if provided, should be at least 100 cm per pig housed.

- *Water allowance*

Age	Pig weights (kg)	Litres/day/per pig
5	7–8	1–2
8	20–22	2–3
12	30–32	4–5

- *Feed Efficiency*   This will depend on the diet but a figure in the range of 1.5 to 1.8 would be a good target to aim for.

Chapter Six

BREEDING POLICY

MAIN OBJECTIVES

THERE ARE three overall objectives which the pig producer must consider and apply throughout all pig production systems.

1. Sow Productivity

This is often measured by the number of pigs weaned or sold per sow per year and is the controlling factor in calculating the output from the herd.

2. Economy of Gain

This factor takes into account growth rate and the efficiency of feed utilisation. Usually measured in liveweight terms, it should be converted to a deadweight figure, using killing out percentage, if pigs are sold on carcase weight.

3. Suitability of Carcase for the Selected Market

This will be measured quantitatively in terms of weight, length, fat depth, fat quality, skin colour and meat quality.

These three objectives have a major impact on the profits of the pig enterprise, as they affect both fixed and variable costs, especially the utilisation of feed which is still the main cost of producing pigmeat.

OBJECTIVES APPLIED TO OUTDOOR PIG PRODUCTION

Females

The physical environment in which the breeding sow is kept is the main factor to be considered when deciding the type of sow needed, and the market environment then dictates the type of boar which will be needed to produce suitable progeny to satisfy market requirements.

For breeding stock that are living and producing in an outdoor environment the year round, the breeding female should be prolific, have good maternal instincts, be independent, quiet and easily handled (lop ears help in this respect). She will need adequate fat reserves to help withstand the rigours of the outdoor life and will generally carry more backfat than the white hybrid sow, to act as an energy store which buffers her against the fluctuating demands of a working life out of doors.

No single breed can meet all these requirements but, by using the Saddleback and Landrace breeds, a first cross 'blue' female can be produced which has most of these qualities and which, in practice, has produced excellent results out of doors. Other breeds which could be combined with the Landrace to produce this outdoor female include the Hampshire and the Duroc.

Boars

The boars used on the outdoor sows will also need to live out of doors. They should be good workers, reasonably aggressive and able to work away on their own, yet quiet enough to live together in a group. A performance tested boar, with good feed efficiency and lower than average backfat, should be selected to help balance the higher fat levels in the 'blue' sow. There is some conflict here between the extra fat which the sow needs for hardiness, and the performance of the slaughter generation. If the progeny are ad-lib fed they will carry excessive backfat; if they are fed on a restricted regime, growth rate suffers. This is the challenge that faces the breeder producing breeding stock for the outdoor herd in the current market environment.

The choice of boar for use on the outdoor sow will nearly always be the Large White, but Sire Line boars are being used to try to meet the specific market demands for quality lean meat.

The new EEC Pig Grading Scheme will come into effect in January 1989 and all slaughter houses will then be obliged to use objective measurements to predict the lean meat content of all slaughter carcases.

REVIEW OF BREEDS

Because of the specific physical and market environments, certain breeds are used in producing breeding stock for the outdoor herd.

The following is not a comprehensive list, but highlights the breeds used at grandparent level to produce the female lines and looks briefly at some breeds used for producing boars which are used to sire the slaughter generation.

British Saddleback (BSB)

The British Saddleback breed was formed in 1968 by the amalgamation of two very old English breeds, the Wessex and the Essex. The Wessex appears to have originated in a cross between the Sussex and Hampshire breeds in the New Forest area of England at the beginning of the nineteenth century. The Wessex Pig Society was formed in 1918 and later incorporated into the National Pig Breeders Association. By this time, the distinctive colour marking of the white saddle over the front shoulder had become a feature of the breed. The Essex takes its name from the county of its origin, and in the early nineteenth century it was crossed with the Neapolitan breed from Italy. The Essex Pig Society was founded in 1918 and the breed was distinguished by colour markings, the ideal being a white saddle over the shoulder and fore-legs with white hind feet and tip of the tail.

In comparison with the Large White and Landrace breeds in England the British Saddleback has not been subjected to any intensive selection and testing programmes by breeders. The Saddleback is a very docile sow, prolific and with strong maternal instincts. Compared with the white breeds, growth rate and feed efficiency are poor, the carcase is long and the loin eye is small. The breed carries a large amount of backfat which supplies more than adequate energy reserves to produce a hardy outdoor sow.

The main contribution of the Saddleback to the outdoor breeding programme is to supply the grandparent male or female for production of the blue female parent gilt.

Hampshire

This American breed is black with a white belt, and its origin can be traced back to breeding stock imported from Hampshire, England, in about 1920. The modern American breed has prick ears, rather than lop as in the British Saddleback. The breed is one of the most numerous in the United States, and a main constituent of the three breed rotational crossing system used for commercial pig production. Hampshires have been exported to many countries from the

United States and importations were made to the United Kingdom in the late 1960s.

The breed is characterised by good growth rate, very good killing out percentage and lean content, with a very large loin eye area.

For these reasons, the breed is regarded in the United States as a Sire Line, since its performance in litter characteristics—on a par with other coloured American breeds—is rather poor when compared with European white dam lines.

Large White

The Large White is probably now more widespread than any other breed in the world. A long history of breed improvement goes back to the eighteenth century, with the work of Robert Bakewell and the Leicester breed. At a later date crossing took place with the Cumberland and Yorkshire breeds and there gradually appeared a Large type and a Middle type. Large Whites first appeared as a distinctive breed class at the Royal Show in 1868.

The currently recognised pure white breeds were first recorded by the National Pig Breeders Association, founded in 1884.

In the last thirty years the Large White has been subject to improvement programmes based on testing and selection by breeders working under the MLC Pig Improvement Scheme, as well as by the breeding companies. There is still much variation in the breed but the Large White is considered by many authorities to be the best all round breed in the world. It is long, with a lean carcase and very good feed efficiency and growth rates.

The sow is prolific and docile, and is crossed with the Landrace to produce an F_1 female, which has been the main commercial female used for pigmeat production in the United Kingdom. The boars, with prick ears, tend to be aggressive, but are good workers. The Large White's main contribution to outdoor pig production is to supply the boar which sires the slaughter generation.

British Landrace

The British Landrace is the second most popular breed in the United Kingdom. The word 'Landrace' means breed of the country, and the British Landrace was imported to England from Sweden in 1953. Since then it has become the second most numerous breed in the United Kingdom. Along with the Large White, the British Landrace has been subject to breed improvement, by testing and selecting, by private breeders and breed organisations.

There is still large variation within the breed, but the Landrace can be regarded as an all round maternal breed which is highly prolific, though not quite so rugged as the Large White. The sow is long, lean and docile. The breed is characterised by good growth rate and feed efficiency, with a lean carcase which has a comparatively low killing out percentage.

The Landrace part in the outdoor breeding programme is to provide the grandparent male or female for production of the F_1 Blue parent female.

Duroc

The Duroc is an American breed with a very distinctive reddish brown colour. Its origins in the United States are reported to be found in importations of Red Guinea from Africa in the 1800s, merged with red pigs from the Iberian Peninsula, and with a contribution from the Berkshire breed, by that time established in the United States.

The Duroc is shorter and more rugged than the European white lines and, as a good all round versatile breed, has been exported to many countries around the world. The breed performs very well out of doors and the female is relatively docile.

Growth rate and feed efficiency are good, with a relatively high killing out percentage and low backfat. Litter size, in line with other United States coloured breeds, is poor when compared with European white maternal lines.

The best use in the outdoor breeding programme would be as an alternative to the Saddleback. There would be a decrease in backfat in the slaughter generation, but there could also be some loss of hardiness, and the reduction in maternal instinct may prove difficult to replace in the operation of the overall system.

CROSS-BREEDING SYSTEM

The breeds mentioned are very different, with different strengths and weaknesses. None of these breeds, used on its own, can meet all the requirements for the outdoor pig system. However, a well-planned cross-breeding programme, by exploiting strengths and hiding weaknesses, can go a long way towards meeting most demands.

When two different breeds are crossed, the cross-bred progeny are more productive than the average of the parental lines. This

Table 6.1   Individual and maternal heterosis

Breeding System	Breed of: Sire	Dam	Proportion of maximum Heterosis: Individual	Maternal	Paternal
1. Pure Breeding LR × LR	A	A	0	0	0
2. Two Breed Cross LR × BSB	A	B	1	0	0
3. Back Crossing (LW × LR) × LW	A	AB	½	1	0
4. Three Line Cross (LR × BSB) × LW	C	AB	1	1	0
5. Four Line Cross Cross-bred boar on cross-bred sow	CD	AB	1	1	1

genetic bonus is called heterosis or hybrid vigour. It is mainly connected with biological fitness, in characteristics such as embryo survival, litter size at birth, post-natal survival and growth rate, age at puberty and libido in males. By using a cross-bred female, and a boar of a third breed, the outdoor producer can utilise the components of heterosis known as individual and maternal heterosis. This is illustrated in table 6.1.

This is an advantage the outdoor producer has over the indoor producer, as the cross-breeding programme for the outdoor pig, using a three-breed combination, achieves a higher level of heterosis than the indoor system which mainly follows a back-crossing system.

This certainly helps the outdoor producer to boost sow productivity in terms of numbers born alive, piglet survival and reduction in breeding intervals. To maximise heterosis, the outdoor producer would need to use an unrelated sire line or cross-bred boar on an F_1 blue female. However, cross breeding should not be concerned only with maximising heterosis, but also with the differences within and between the breeds that make up the crossing system.

CHOICE OF REPLACEMENT BREEDING STOCK

Previous discussions on basic policy decisions in Chapter Two indicated that there are two ways of producing replacement breeding females, either through a home-bred system or by buying in replacement females. These options will now be discussed in greater detail, using a 480-sow outdoor unit as a model for numbers required to maintain herd size and pig flow.

Home-Bred Replacements

This system involves the producer in maintaining a small purebred herd of Saddleback grandparent (GP) sows, which are mated with Landrace GP boars to produce a regular supply of home bred, first cross, blue gilts. This is called a Closed Herd Multiplier (CHM) and pure bred replacements for the GP herds would be bought from a nucleus breeder or breeding organisation. The roles of the Closed Herd Multiplier breeds could be reversed, maintaining a female Landrace herd with Saddleback boars. Alternatively, Landrace semen through artificial insemination could be used on Saddleback females.

Figure 6.1 shows in diagrammatic form how the Closed Herd Multiplier works, based on a policy of buying in grandparent gilts and grandparent boars, and using parent boars for siring the slaughter generation.

A small herd of GP sows, about forty in number, would be mated to GP boars. About twenty replacement GPs would be needed each year. Farrowing should be spread throughout the year to maintain a regular flow of selected females to the commercial herd. The multiplier herd could be run outdoors alongside the main herd, or could be housed separately indoors. This decision would depend to some extent on choice of breed for female GPs.

Calculations for replacements are based on a total of eight hundred pigs produced in the Closed Herd Multiplier, 50 per cent of which would be gilts, providing four hundred gilts to choose from each year. With a selection rate of 60 per cent, this could provide up to 240 selected females for the commercial herd each year. A 480- to 500-sow commercial herd, with a replacement rate of 40 per cent, will require about two hundred gilts per year.

This is an attractive proposition for the larger outdoor producer, and can easily be scaled up in size to deal with a larger sow population. Continuous genetic improvement can be maintained by linking to a reputable nucleus herd which is known to be making genetic progress.

The cash outlay for buying replacements for only the CHM will certainly be lower, and the number of replacement females being

Plate 14   Metal fender showing method of attachment to farrowing hut.

Plate 15   Double farrowing huts manufactured out of plywood.

Plate 16 Specially designed boar ark.

Plate 17 Dry sow ark in gestation paddock.

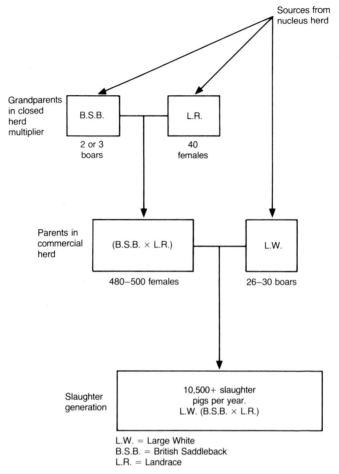

Figure 6.1   The closed herd multiplier.

brought on to the farm from outside is very much reduced, which may be beneficial to the health of the enterprise.

There are, however, many complications. There is some loss of productivity, because not all of the sows in the enterprise are first cross sows mated to a third breed. This carries some financial consequences, which have to be taken into account. A separate multiplier herd site may be required, and running a CHM may be easier for a herd run totally indoors. The purebred sows need careful mating and follow-through of gilts up to selection. Keeping up a regular flow of gilts for the commercial herd to maintain mating patterns frequently proves to be a problem area. In practice, these management complications lead, in most situations, to the practical day-to-day disadvantages outweighing the theoretical advantages.

Purchasing all Replacement Parent Gilts and Boars

The alternative system is to buy in all cross-bred parent gilts from one multiplier herd, and tested parent boars from the nucleus in the same closed breeding pyramid. This is the most effective genetic solution, with continuous genetic improvement coming from the nucleus herd with genetic improvement lag reduced to a minimum period of about two and a half years. Cross breeding advantage is maximised through having all first cross sows. Figure 6.2 shows this in diagrammatic form.

This replacement system requires sixteen or seventeen gilts to be brought in monthly, giving a total of two hundred in the year. Gilts can be slotted into the herd mating pattern with few management complications. This approach allows the staff to concentrate entirely on the business of commercial pig production without the added distraction of running a separate breeding programme. Most commercial units take in replacement gilts when they are 5½ to 6 months old, but if the integration of maiden gilts causes health problems, a practical alternative is to take in selected weaner gilts at between 30 and 35 kilogrammes liveweight. With suitable acclimatisation, these weaner gilts can be grown on to a suitable weight for service and integrated into the main herd at the appropriate time.

Replacement Rates

Gilts
Total numbers required are similar whether homebred or purchased. A new unit will need to budget for 7 to 10 per cent replacements in the first year, 15 to 20 per cent in the second year, and around 40 to 45 per cent even running. This will give a life in the breeding herd of two and a half to three and a half years, with an average of six to eight litters in a working lifetime. With weaning at about three weeks rather than at four to five weeks, a sow's working lifetime in the herd will be reduced. Replacing the female herd over a two to three year period keeps up the genetic improvement and should promote a herd profile which maintains the correct balance of sows and gilts, and old and young sows, in the herd. Sow mortality on outdoor units runs at about 2 to 2½ per cent, which is

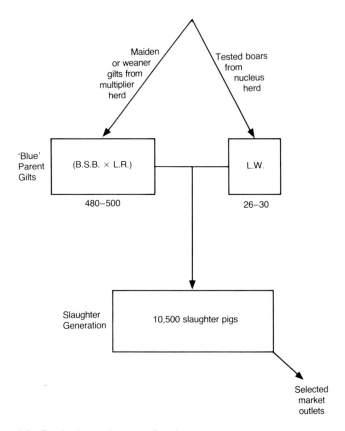

Figure 6.2   Purchasing replacement females as parents.

lower than on indoor units, and there will be culling of non-productive sows, mainly lame or barren, or because of age. Those producers purchasing weaner gilts at 30 kg will need to make an allowance for some mortality and for non-selected animals breeding at age, to meet these targets.

Boars
Boars should be bought when they are five to six months of age and then acclimatised to the unit. If possible, they should be mixed in a working group before delivery. Because of the working and management methods, outdoor units will have a higher boar to sow ratio than indoor herds. Some boars will always be in use in the in-pig

sow paddocks to check groups of sows for return to service. Vasectomised boars may be used as 'chasers' with groups of gilts, and this may reduce working boar requirements. Overall, a ratio of six to seven boars per one hundred sows would be a good working target. Larger herds may be able to operate slightly below this figure, and a five hundred sow unit should have a target of twenty-six to twenty-eight working boars. Boars will need replacing after eighteen months' to two years' working life in the herd, but the new boars coming in will help in keeping up with the pace of genetic improvement in the nucleus herd. Size and overweight will be the usual reasons for replacement because as those working in outside units are fed alongside newly weaned sows, it is difficult to restrict their individual feed intake. A five hundred sow unit should budget to replace half its boars each year, so that fourteen or fifteen boars will need to be scheduled for replacement each year, with delivery spread throughout the year.

Artificial Insemination

AI is used very successfully on a number of outdoor units. This provides access to high-pointed, performance-tested boars from MLC and a number of other organisations.

A special area will be needed in which sows can be confined during insemination. Facilities will be required to store and clean equipment. AI will often be used alongside natural service, and entire and vasectomised boars will help in stimulation of oestrus.

The balance between AI and natural service can be varied according to the workload in any particular week. This can be very helpful if a large number of sows are weaned in one batch, and when a number of working boars are out of action because of size, lameness or refusal to work.

SOURCES OF BREEDING STOCK

A number of breeders and breeding organisations have set out to supply the market for outdoor gilts, but the choice for boars is even wider. Price, guarantees, product quality, health policy, availability and back-up services will need to be taken into account before a decision to purchase is made.

Information from individual producers, surveys and recording schemes indicates that the most popular choice for replacement of breeding stock is to buy in gilts and tested boars from the breeding companies. The reputable companies have been involved in testing and selection, in some cases for over twenty years. In these organisations breeds have been improved and changed, and lines developed for specific purposes and market outlets. The next few years will see the development and marketing of distinctive lines of pigs, drawn from current breeds, some of which may be synthetic lines. This follows patterns already established in the poultry breeding world, with the breeders marketing specially developed lines for commercial egg and broiler meat production. We can anticipate similar changes in the pig breeding world, and no doubt the market for outdoor pigs will be an area for special attention.

A list of sources of breeding stock is set out in a special section at the end of this book.

Chapter Seven

LABOUR AND STAFFING

INTRODUCTION

ANYONE WHO WORKS full time with livestock tends to be a special type of person, and working with pigs out of doors makes very specific demands. Since there are not very many outdoor units, not many staff are involved in this work. My estimate is that the total will probably be less than 5 per cent of all managers and stockmen working in the pig industry, really just a handful of people.

Setting out a list of skills, knowledge and attributes to be sought in an employee is relatively easy compared with finding the person to match up to them, and the employer has his part to play, as will be discussed shortly.

Throughout this book I have used the term 'stockman' in referring to staff looking after pigs. I am aware that there are a number of successful female owners and females managing and working on outdoor units. The term 'stockperson' is rather cumbersome, and where I have used the word 'stockman' I mean both male and female staff working in pig production.

REQUIREMENTS FOR OUTDOOR STOCKMEN

These requirements are not set out in order of importance. It is unlikely that any one person will fulfil all of them, and a balance of the various attributes is the best that can be hoped for.

Stockmanship and Pig Husbandry

A thorough knowledge of the pig is essential, and there is no substitute for good old-fashioned stockmanship. This should be matched with an understanding of the basic scientific principles of pig production.

A Concern for the Welfare of the Stock

A sympathetic approach to the pig, and concern for its comfort and welfare, are an integral part of stockmanship. Welfare is not just for pigs in confinement, and the outdoor stockman has a key role to play in this area.

Knowledge of the System

Knowledge of and confidence in the system are essential, with a determination that the system can and will work.

Outdoor Environment

By definition and choice of job the stockman will be working out of doors in all weather. Rain, wind, snow and cold temperatures are the discomforts that come first to mind, but are these worse than the hot, sunny days we get in summer? An all weather person is called for.

Physical Fitness

The outdoor job is a physical one, especially when related to the conditions outlined above. There is lots of carrying, and driving of both livestock and vehicles. (Keeping fit on the job could be considered a benefit, with little need for jogging after work!)

Decision Making

There is need, in all aspects of livestock production, to take and make decisions on the spot—possibly more so than in any other occupation. The outdoor herd may be distant from base, and decisions will have to be made quickly, frequently without a second opinion.

Teamwork

Staff working with outdoor pigs are usually part of an extended team that stretches beyond their everyday colleagues. Staff from the arable section of the farm will fall into this category, along with part-time help, and an occasional contribution from the boss!

Knowledge of Machinery and Equipment

Outdoor pig production has its own set of equipment and machinery that must function at all times or the whole business will come to a halt. Tractors and other vehicles must start every day, all the year round. Knowledge of the operation of electric fencing is another necessary skill, along with the ability to keep the water supply moving.

Recording of Physical Performance

Recording of breeding stock performance, in conditions that are frequently less than ideal, is a most important part of the job. (At least there is no danger that a vital diary of the week's records can be dropped down the slats.)

Family Support

The outdoor stockman often works unsocial hours, and may be away from home for the greater part of the day. Family support not only makes life easier, but will help to improve performance, and it often proves helpful if the spouse can be employed on the farm, at least part time. Last but not least, a sense of humour will help things along—but this requirement is not specific to those working with outdoor pigs.

What About the Employer?

So much for a wish list for the employee, but what about the ideal employer? He or she is unlikely to exist in the business of outdoor pig production—or any other for that matter. A complementary list of requirements can be drawn up, and for a starter I list ten priority areas.

Provide a Suitable Framework

The employer must establish a suitable framework and background for the running of the enterprise. By this I mean strong leadership, suitable motivation, and an atmosphere and environment which inspires trust and confidence. Good personal communication is essential to keep the business heading comfortably in the right direction.

Indicate Specific Requirements

A written job description, setting out conditions of work, responsibilities and duties for individual employees, provides a good basis for a working relationship.

Targets

In addition to the job description, the staff should be aware of overall physical performance targets over specific time periods. Results should be compared to targets, which are reviewed and up-dated as necessary. It is even better if overall financial targets can be linked with herd performance.

Physical Needs

These needs will depend on the specific job, and will differ for a manager and for a member of his team. The list may include domestic housing, vehicles, telephones—two-way radios?—suitable office and changing and toilet area.

Time Off

All employees need time away from the job, and this should be planned ahead as far as possible. Included in the plan are weekend arrangements, holidays, dental and medical check-ups, and family and school demands.

Broader Horizons?

Well-motivated staff will be keen to take an opportunity for further training to increase their skills. This may be through day-release, on-the-job training, or special courses and seminars away from the farm. Also included should be discussion groups, visits to other farms, and trade fairs, so long as this does not present a health risk. The end result may be internal promotion within the farm or a move away to a more senior position on another unit. Although this may seem to be an immediate loss, it should be seen as success in helping a member of staff towards achieving his personal goals and ambitions in life. Better to have high-quality, well-motivated staff than a team of mediocre time-servers.

Rewards

Many of the rewards of doing a job have been mentioned, but the first one that usually comes to mind is cash. Specific recommendations cannot be made about rates of pay, but in my experience a rate for the job well done, paid weekly or monthly, is better than a series of performance linked bonus payments, which frequently lead to disappointment for both parties. Ability, experience and track record will all need to be taken into consideration in arriving at salary rate, as well as the size, scope and nature of the job. Not at all easy, but all the benefits and advantages of the job should be considered, rather than just cash in pocket.

Family support

The employee, especially in the countryside, should be considered not just as an individual, but as part of a family. Rural living makes special demands on wives and children, as well as bringing benefits, and this must be understood and given a sympathetic approach by the employer, regarding both work and leisure time.

Job Satisfaction

This is difficult to define, but is a combination of many of the topics already discussed. Increasing knowledge, skill and monetary rewards are all a part, but a good measure of personal responsibility, credit for good work, and confirmation of a job well done are major components of job satisfaction for the employee who is really committed to his work.

Performance Review

'How am I doing on the job?' is a frequent question. It needs to be answered on an informal basis, at least twice a year, and makes a good opportunity for the exchange of views, discussion of problem areas, and putting forward suggestions on either side.

INDOORS OR OUTDOORS?

A difficult choice to make (see page 100), and all depends on personal likes and dislikes. One last word—one other hazard for many outdoor men is danger from low-flying aircraft!

Situation	Indoors	Outdoors
The work place	Dry, warm under cover	Extremes of climate and all weathers
Distance	Compact layout	Large distances, sometimes remote
Working hours	Fairly well-defined working pattern	Some unsocial hours
Recording	Office and computer	Diary and notebook initially
Special skills	Ventilation and mechanical equipment	Pig movement, vehicle servicing, electric fencing
Problem areas	Dust, noise and smell. Slurry handling, power washing. Herd health	Labour peaks at paddock resiting. Rogue sows, moving and catching pigs
Special hazards	Power failures, visiting salesmen	Prolonged frosts, trespassers, rustling and security
Special advantages	Warm showers and change of working clothing	Time spent outdoors in good weather

How Many Staff Required?

This is a difficult question to answer, as it will depend on herd size, the details of the production system, and the degree of integration with other farm staff. As a general rule, one man and some part-time help will cope relatively easily with 130 to 150 sows, raising weaners to the point of sale at 30 kg. A three-man team will be needed to operate a 480-sow unit with weaners transferred off the field at three to four weeks of age. Some additional help may be needed at peak times, such as straw stacking, or for moving animals on to fresh ground. Actual staffing levels will have to be worked out for each farm when all the various factors and circumstances have been taken into account.

TRAINING—ON AND OFF THE FARM

On the Farm

It is best to take a broad view of this. Outdoor pig producers have been keen and willing to provide their own training on the farm, especially in some large organisations which may have several commercial pig units. This on the job training is first class, and can be backed up by meetings, discussion groups, seminars and open days. There are a number of good technical reports and surveys, and the volume of information available is growing. Feed and breeding companies are a good source of information on management techniques and new methods. A few consultants now specialise in setting up and operating outdoor pig systems.

Agricultural Training Board

The Agricultural Training Board runs a series of courses for staff involved in pig production. They are mainly directed towards basic husbandry skills, but there are also courses in man management, supervision and training on the farm.

The ATB are currently preparing special courses and training in outdoor pig production.

Agricultural Colleges

A number of agricultural colleges offer special courses in pig husbandry, and some colleges operate their own outdoor units as part of their teaching syllabus and training.

Berkshire College of Agriculture has two commercial pig units, one indoor and one outdoor; the college offers two advanced courses with options in pig production.

Chapter Eight

SOME HEALTH CONSIDERATIONS

INTRODUCTION

IT IS NOT the intention, in this chapter, to string together a long list of pig diseases, their diagnosis, treatment, and control. This information is already available in many competent and authoritative veterinary publications. A list of recommended reading and references will be found in a special section at the end of this book.

Research and investigation work on health control methods continues on a world-wide basis and is increasing our knowledge of pig diseases and their prevention. There is at present very little written information on health considerations for outdoor systems, but a valuable contribution is included in Volume 18 of the *Pig Veterinary Society Proceedings*, which has a number of papers on outdoor pig keeping.

Good health is a vital component of outdoor pig production, and maintaining health standards involves a complex balance between breeding, management and nutrition, backed up by a strong veterinary contribution.

As a general observation, outdoor breeding herds in the United Kingdom appear to have a better health record than do indoor herds. This applies particularly to the larger outdoor herds where effective disease control methods have been set up and followed.

The reasons for this better health record are not immediately clear, but the variable outdoor environment can be turned to advantage by good stockmanship and positive management. Outdoor sows appear to have fewer respiratory problems than those housed indoors, and in most outdoor situations there is less stress on sows and gilts.

Outdoor sows living in small groups and well supplied with straw bedding are likely to be more comfortable than sows housed indoors. Their freedom of movement and access to fresh air and exercise provides a more natural way of keeping pigs than some intensive systems.

Regular herd movement to clean ground must be considered as a major contribution to the maintenance of herd health. Movement of the herd to clean ground helps to avoid build-up of parasites and limits the problems that arise from poaching of the ground and build-up of mud. The herd should stay on the same ground for a maximum of two years, but a shorter period would be better. One way that this can be achieved is by moving half of the herd each year. Outdoor herds which do not have sufficient ground to follow a planned rotation to clean ground on a regular basis will have great difficulty in maintaining adequate health standards.

POSITIVE HEALTH CONTROL

Financial records from a number of sources confirm lower veterinary and medicine costs for outdoor herds than for indoor herds. Annual veterinary costs per breeding sow in an outdoor herd are shown, in both the Cambridge and Exeter reports, to be about half those in comparable indoor herds, and this has been a fairly consistent feature in recent years.

For the individual commercial producer, a successful health control policy will help to prevent disease and reduce the financial losses that disease might cause. Loss of profit is incurred in several ways:

- The reduced performance in animals, especially reproductive performance.
- Direct loss of breeding stock and suckling pigs.
- Unpredictable performance results in less than optimum use of facilities and equipment, and other fixed cost items.
- Direct cost of treatment—drugs, medicines and extra veterinary input.

Specific figures are difficult to work out, as each farm situation is different. The cost of disease will depend on the severity of the outbreak and the method of dealing with it. Table 8.1, taken from Volume 17 of the *Pig Veterinary Society Proceedings* illustrates how, in a 100-sow herd, the effects of various changes would affect the theoretical profit.

A positive health-control policy, based on disease prevention, is an integral part of both indoor and outdoor pig production, and the consultant veterinarian has a central role to play in establishing and operating a successful routine.

Table 8.1   Effects of changing parameters on the theoretical profit of a pig farm

	Change	Profit	% Change
Feed cost £150.00 to £165.00 per tonne	+ 10%	£12,000	− 40%
F.C.E. 2.7 : 1 to 3 : 1	+ 11%	£12,000	− 40%
Sale price £70.00 to £73.50	+ 5%	£27,000	+ 35%
Fattening mortality 2.5% to 5%	+ 100%	£19,500	− 2.5%
Litter size (alive) 10.5 to 11	+ 48%	£21,000	+ 5%
Farrowing rate 90% to 75%	− 17%	£16,410	− 18%

100 sow herd   Selling 2,000 pigs/year
£10 profit/pig   £70 sale price
Profit £20,000 per year

THE ROLE OF THE VETERINARY ADVISER

With increasing specialisation in pig production, a number of veterinary consultants have emerged in both the indoor and the outdoor disciplines. To obtain maximum benefit from their knowledge and skills, the outdoor producer should work with them on a consultative basis in a number of ways.

Setting up a Unit or Expanding an Existing One

It is extremely valuable to have the veterinary adviser sit in on initial discussions at the planning phase of development. Key areas include site location, sources of stock and integration programmes.

Site Location

Exact location of a potential site in relation to other pig enterprises is a fundamental consideration. Sites near existing units should be avoided as disease can travel quickly between farms, carried by birds or vermin. Wind-borne diseases can travel over long distances, and use should be made of natural barriers such as hills and wooded areas. Busy roads carrying pigs for slaughter should be avoided, as there is a potential risk from transmissible gastro-enteritis (TGE) and a number of other diseases.

Sources of Breeding Stock

The veterinary adviser will play an important part in helping to select a suitable source of breeding stock in the case of a new unit or replacement stock policy for an existing unit. It is important to establish the health status of the source of breeding stock, so that a new herd can be confidently established with the healthiest stock available. There should be no compromise in this area: the basic rule is to establish a clean herd and then protect the herd from chance introduction of disease.

Liaison between the producer's veterinarian and the veterinarian advising the supply source of breeding stock is essential. In this way, objective information can be exchanged on a professional basis, and with the combined specialist knowledge of the purchaser and his veterinary surgeon an overall assessment can be made about the suitability of the stock for the proposed enterprise. A change of supply source may be necessary from time to time, at which stage the veterinary input is essential.

Integration and Acclimatisation of Breeding Stock

This follows on from purchase of breeding stock, and some general guidelines on this topic follow in a later section. Specific recommendations can be set out by the consultant veterinarian according to the health status of the incoming stock and the health of the breeding stock on the recipient farm.

Herd Visits for Clinical Inspection

Herd visits will be made on a regular advisory basis rather than as an emergency 'fire brigade' remedy. Visits often take place monthly, but at least quarterly. This provides a good opportunity for a clinical inspection of the stock alongside the manager and staff. Problem solving can begin with inspection of performance and health records, and on-the-spot advice can be given in the field.

Records play a fundamental part in the veterinary adviser's visits, and a number of veterinarians operate their own computerised recording schemes—but seeing the pigs on the ground is all important.

Back-up Service

In addition to recording and clinical inspection, many veterinary advisers will offer a wide range of other services. These will include diagnostic facilities in their own lab or through veterinary investigation centres, and post-mortem work in the field, at the lab, or in

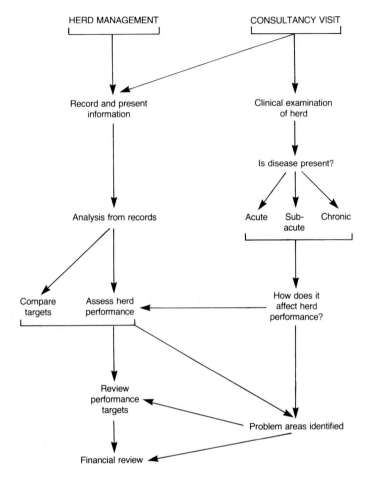

Figure 8.1   Combined management and veterinary approach to problem solving.

the slaughterhouse. The veterinarian is also a link to many other specialists, both veterinary and non-veterinary, working in pig production, which brings a multi-disciplinary approach to outdoor pig production.

Overall, regular objective appraisal of the outdoor herd by an experienced veterinarian can provide a unique opportunity to exchange information on a wide range of topics, and can enhance communications between staff, owner, and all the various parties involved in the business of running an outdoor pig unit.

Vaccination Programme

The veterinary consultant, from his knowledge of the farm and breeding stock, will recommend a specific vaccination programme as part of the overall health control programme. Drug usage, strategic medication and parasite control would all fall into this category.

INTEGRATION AND ACCLIMATISATION

Introduction

Introduction and acclimatisation of breeding stock has become a significant topic in recent years, with the rapid development of breeding organisations and a market situation in which the vast majority of commercial producers buy in all or part of their replacement breeding stock on a regular basis. Most outdoor producers buy in breeding boars, parent gilts as maidens or weaners, and occasionally grandparent males and females.

Acclimatisation can be defined as the adjustment of the breeding pig to the conditions prevailing on the farm to which it has been introduced, to enable it to perform to optimum standards.

Background to Disease Levels

It should be noted that pigs carry a widely varying range of infectious agents. Some of these may be unimportant, some harmful and potentially dangerous, and some to be kept out at any price.

Careful acclimatisation and integration of new breeding stock will take all these considerations into account, and practical experience should be backed up by specific veterinary advice and recommendations.

In practice, each breeding herd will develop its own population of organisms which will differ in species, type and concentration from farm to farm. When pigs from different sources are mixed together, the mixing of these varying microflora can result in the appearance of clinical disease or the raising of sub-clinical disease to significant levels. When breeding stock are moved from one herd to another, the introduced pigs will have to establish an immunity to the organisms endemic in the recipient herd if they do not already have such immunity.

It should also be remembered that pigs in the recipient herd have to establish an immunity to any new organisms being brought in by the new pigs.

Immunity

Careful acclimatisation and integration will provide protection in both directions by building up immunity before the pigs are mixed. This is known as 'acquired immunity' and is brought about by the pigs contracting a mild infection which they combat by producing antibodies. The antibodies multiply in the bloodstream, building up immunity levels. This process will take at least three weeks and may take up to several months. With female breeding stock, immunity is built up and passed on, through colostrum, to suckling pigs. Immunity can be built up within the herd, and there are a number of well-developed methods by which the acquired immune status of incoming breeding stock can be enhanced.

Methods

Breeding stock can be brought in at three different stages:

- Maiden gilts at 95 to 105 kg liveweight.
- Breeder weaners at approximately 30–35 kg liveweight.
- Boars at 5½ to 6 months of age.

Sources of Stock

The most important consideration is to buy breeding stock from a reputable source, after consultation between the veterinarians advising each party, as described earlier. Ideally, breeding stock should be bought from a closed pyramid, with boars from the nucleus herd and gilts from a multiplier herd within the same closed pyramid. Replacements should come from the same supply herds, so that the commercial outdoor herd is firmly and directly linked to what is, in effect, a safe source of genetically improved and healthy breeding stock.

Transport and Delivery

Special attention should be paid to hygiene and sanitation in transport and delivery. Trucks and drivers should be 'clean' and breeding stock should be delivered directly from the source farm wherever this is possible.

Maiden Gilts

These should be placed in isolated clean paddocks, which can also be used for training purposes. Shade should be provided, with access to clean water, and they should be kept in isolation and under close observation as they settle in and recover from transport and mixing stress. To help them acquire their own active immunity, piglet dung and scour from the farrowing section of the main herd should then be placed in the paddock. This process can be repeated several times with fresh material, say twice weekly. This is known as 'feedback', and to strengthen the acquisition of immunity some producers introduce small cull sows, which are about to leave the breeding herd, into the gilt paddocks, but this should not be done until a few days after delivery to allow the new stock to settle down. This can be repeated two or three times, and helps incoming gilts to build up their acquired immunity fairly quickly.

Close observation of gilts is essential in this period, with particular attention to appetite levels, coughing, discharges or scouring. Gilts showing signs of distress, or which are persistently off colour, should be treated according to veterinary advice.

An integration period of at least four to five weeks is required. This will allow gilts not only to build up immunity, but also to train to the electric fence, and to acquire condition before mating. Signs of oestrus will be observed and should be recorded. Vasectomised boars can be used to stimulate heat, and further information is provided on vasectomised boars later in this chapter. Gilts should be mated when they are about 210 to 220 days of age, and in the weight range between 115 and 125 kg liveweight, probably at their third or fourth heat cycle, so a group of boars must be introduced ahead of this time. All these events have to be telescoped into a relatively short period if gilts are to be mated and drafted into the main breeding herd on time to meet performance targets.

Weaner Gilts

To allow more time for these procedures, and to give a longer acclimatisation period, many larger outdoor producers follow a policy of buying in weaner gilts at about 30 to 35 kg liveweight. This can also be a sound policy where there is a health problem in the recipient herd, making a longer period of acclimatisation desirable.

Most producers take delivery of weaner gilts when they are about 30 to 35 kg liveweight. As described in the earlier management section, they are often housed initially in straw yards. They will of course come indirectly into contact with the rest of the herd from the time of delivery, but active integration begins when they are moved out into the paddocks at about 50 to 60 kg liveweight. The feedback system is used in a similar way to the maiden gilts' treatment, with dung, scour, and cull sows, but it can be continued for a longer period. This immunisation procedure should stop ten to fourteen days before mating, as the gilts should be fully acclimatised by this time.

Boars

Introduction   The introduction of tested boars to the outdoor unit needs careful management. These boars have been reared away from females on a strict test regime, and will most likely have been fed on meal or pellets in a trough. Handling, integration and acclimatisation of the young boar must be undertaken with care and understanding.

Pre Delivery   As most boars in outdoor units work in groups, it is advisable to ask the breeder to mix the boars after they come off test and before delivery. Some breeding organisations will then feed them as a group, with nuts or cobs, to familiarise them with the feeding system in the commercial herd. Boars will often be available for delivery at around 5½ to 6 months of age. The number of boars will depend on the size of the breeding herd and the number of sows in each group at weaning. Service techniques vary between farms, but young boars will most often be mixed into groups of three or occasionally four. If necessary these group sizes can be broken down to fit the particular farm circumstances.

On Delivery   The new group of boars should be kept separate from the other pigs for the first seven to ten days, preferably in a dry paddock with shade and which must also be used for training with the electric fence. This allows time for observation of the incoming stock, and for making sure that they are not incubating any disease which could cause problems.

Acclimatisation   The feedback procedure should be followed as for maiden gilts, under veterinary guidance, for a period of three to four weeks, with careful observation, and treatment if necessary.

Integration and Use   After the period of acclimatisation the group can be moved into contact with the rest of the breeding herd. A period of training should follow, and this was described in detail in an earlier chapter. The age of boars at first service will be between seven and eight months. They should not be overworked for the first few months, beginning with two or three services per week and building up to a full working rate of five or six matings per week when they are about one year old. This work rate can be controlled by careful introduction and removal of young boars into and out of the service paddocks. Boar to sow ratio will need to be carefully adjusted to take into account the young boars and the number of females in the group to be mated.

Because of the group weaning and group mating system used in outdoor systems, outdoor herds always carry more boars than an indoor herd of a similar size. Boar to sow ratio on the indoor herd will usually run at one boar to twenty sows, but in outdoor herds at about one boar to thirteen or fourteen sows.

Most young boars will work straight away, but some may need guidance and supervision in the early stages. Gilts or small sows should be used in the training period and extra time and effort spent by staff with young boars at this stage is time well spent.

Acclimatisation and integration of replacement stock is a very important part of the health control policy of the outdoor herd. All incoming breeding stock should follow the specific pattern recommended by the veterinary consultant. This will help to maintain a healthy herd, and provide replacement breeding stock at the right time and stage to help meet performance and financial targets.

Vasectomised Boars

Vasectomised boars are used by a number of pig producers in both outdoor and indoor systems. The original concept in pigs dates back about twenty years to research work carried out at Nottingham University by Dr Cole and Dr Brooks, when they were examining factors influencing the attainment of puberty in the gilt. They found that one of the main factors influencing the onset of puberty was the actual presence of boars running with the group of gilts. This was much more effective than just sight, sound and smell. Vasectomised boars were used in the experiment, and the use of this type of boar for stimulating heat in groups of gilts has gradually increased on commercial units over the years.

The method is particularly useful since it allows the producer to use a relatively cheap male pig to run with groups of females. Sight, sound, smell, presence, and behaviour pattern are all provided, and newly weaned sows and groups of gilts can be given maximum boar contact, with a reduced risk of injury, wear and tear, and overwork of the high-priced, tested working boars. Use of the vasectomised boars may also help to reduce fighting when sows are grouped together at weaning. A young vasectomised boar that has been working in the main herd may also be used to help with integration of incoming gilts, in building up their herd immunity.

Plate 18   Sows in gestation paddock enjoying the use of their wallow.

Plate 19   Sows inspecting wallow bath.

Plate 20   Siting of water to provide ready access for lactating sows is important.

Plate 21   Home-made water drinker, robust and functional.

The operation is a relatively simple one, and can be carried out on the farm by a veterinarian, using an anaesthetic. The spermatic cord is exposed through incisions, and the vas deferens is isolated, tied in two places, and then cut between the knots.

The operation will normally be carried out when the boar is five to six months of age, but he will not be fully effective until he reaches ten months, when he starts to produce pheromones, which play an important part in stimulation of oestrus.

The vasectomised boars will need to be replaced regularly, as they put on weight fairly quickly, and they must follow the integration and health procedures if they are brought into the unit from outside. Although he will not be able to get females pregnant, the vasectomised boar is, by all other standards, a working boar, and he should be handled and treated with as much respect and care as a normal herd boar.

In practice, many large-scale outdoor units will maintain a small team of three or four vasectomised boars, with a spread in age and weight range that will allow them to be used with incoming gilts or as chasers in the gestation paddocks.

HERD HEALTH PROGRAMME

Introduction

As indicated previously, the veterinary consultant should recommend a herd vaccination programme. This vaccination policy would depend to a large extent on the current disease status of the herd and the likely disease risk. Blanket recommendations cannot be given, but the following guidelines can be set out.

Vaccination Programme

Vaccinations are certain to be advised for swine erysipelas. Other vaccines used most frequently include:

- Porcine Parvovirus
- *E. Coli*—for neo-natal and milk scours in young pigs
- *Clostridium perfringens* Type II.

Frequency and timing would depend on veterinary advice. Boars should also be included in this programme, a point which is frequently overlooked.

Parasite Control

Management and health routines can be devised for the outdoor breeding herd which eliminate or minimise the problems that can arise from a number of parasites. A number of organisations produce breeding stock for sale that were derived from primary hysterectomy procedures and which are clean and free from internal and external parasites. The best solution of course is to buy from these sources and then to take the necessary precautions to keep them clean.

Mange
Mange should not be a problem if breeding stock are bought from a clean source. However, if mange is present, some form of mange wash or dressing will need to be applied regularly for both sows and boars. A very effective injection is now available which controls mange mite.

Worms
Starting off clean and following up by a rotation of paddocks should prevent a worm build-up in the breeding herd. Where problems are encountered it may be necessary to treat by individual dosing or, more frequently, by medication through the feed, or by injection.

Lice
A number of long-established outdoor herds are affected by the pig louse. Dusting or washing with a suitable compound is the best method of treatment, but to be fully effective may need several repeat treatments.

Control of parasites has a beneficial effect on both pig comfort and physical performance, and is a major consideration in pig health. The best method is to start off with clean stock.

MANAGEMENT AND HEALTH INTERACTIONS

In all types of pig production there is a relationship between management and health, and this is particularly true with outdoor systems. The level of disease found in the outdoor herd can largely be determined by the quality of management, and many potential health hazards can be headed off by careful husbandry and dedicated stockmanship. Some problems can quickly get out of control and lead to herd health problems unless they are dealt with promptly.

Lameness and Injury

Feet and legs are always at risk with outdoor breeding stock, and much will depend on ground conditions. With deep mud or flinty stones problems can be expected, especially in service paddocks. This situation highlights the importance of choosing the right type of ground conditions for outdoor pigs; the wrong choice may lead to a breakdown in the system.

Lameness in the adult breeding stock may be caused by swine erysipelas in its chronic form. This is caused by localisation of the bacteria in hip, back and knee joints. The affected joint becomes swollen and after a period of three to four weeks firms up, causing stiffness, leading to lameness. These problems can be avoided by following a regular vaccination programme, not forgetting to treat the boars as well as the female breeding stock.

Feet and claws of pigs can be affected in a number of ways. Physical damage or injury to the hoof or wall of the claw may be followed by lesions, which in turn provide entry for secondary bacterial infections. Routine treatment for feet can be given by running adult breeding stock through a suitable footbath containing five to ten per cent formalin or five per cent copper sulphate solution. Affected pigs may need repeat treatment, running them through two or three times in a seven to ten day period.

Foot problems should be dealt with immediately. Breeding stock that are reluctant to get up and move about should have their feet examined. Individual treatment may be necessary, with injection of antibiotic under veterinary supervision, and local wounds and lesions treated with a suitable spray.

It is also well worth while checking on biotin levels in the feed, as biotin deficiency has been identified in some herds which have foot and lameness problems. Supplementation of the diet should be in the range of 130 to 150 mg per tonne, which should provide more than adequate levels.

Boars are particularly susceptible to sprains and strains, so they should be carefully watched for signs of overwork and lameness. In some cases rest may be necessary, and for total recovery some form of antibiotic treatment may be needed.

Heatstroke and Sunburn

These conditions can affect pigs quite quickly, especially newly delivered breeding stock and sows immediately after farrowing.

The pig has poor heat regulation mechanisms, with little protection from hair, and is unable to sweat except through the mouth. As temperatures rise above 25°C to 30°C, signs of distress quickly become apparent. Adult breeding stock will salivate, pant with the mouth wide open and breathe with difficulty. Sunburn will affect first of all the skin behind the ears, and the udder, followed by the back and flanks. Sunburn can be severe enough in gilts and sows to prevent mating, and can stop boars working. Heat stroke can lead to prostration, and in severe cases to death. Temporary relief may be given by use of tranquillisers, but prevention by provision of shade and wallows is the best solution.

Shade
Mention has already been made, in the chapter on management, of the provision of shade and wallows. In the unpredictable climate of the United Kingdom they should be set up early in the year, otherwise a few unexpected early days of hot sunshine can cause problems.

Most outdoor units have little or no natural shade, and farrowing and gestation huts become extremely hot inside, so artificial shade must be provided. The roof is the most important feature. Strong upright wooden poles supporting camouflage netting or some other lightweight material that does not conduct heat too easily will do the job. Other roofing materials that can be used include strips of wood or fencing panels that will help to break up the direct radiant heat from the sun. Big bales can be used to build a temporary wall, which will give effective shade.

Wallows
Wallows can be made, or sows encouraged to create their own, somewhere near the water supply. The pig likes to be almost fully submerged in the wallow, and to have a layer of caked mud on its skin when it is not submerged. Mud is more effective than clean water since much more moisture is retained and, as a result, evaporation continues for a much longer period. Heat loss from the body can be increased by variation of the lying position, to allow the greatest area of skin to be submerged. Sufficient length and depth should be allowed, in natural or artificial wallows, for the sow or boar to do this, so helping to prevent heat stress and hyperthermia.

A specially made wallow bath typically would be made of galvanised steel sheeting, with an attached covered service box controlling the water supply. Overall measurements would be in the range 2.0 m × 1.35 m, and between 225 and 250 mm deep.

Seasonal Infertility

Seasonal infertility is a term used to describe poor reproductive performance by the breeding herd in the late summer months. It occurs in a number of countries around the world, in both the northern and southern hemispheres, and was first reported by Stork in the United Kingdom in 1979. Similar investigations and findings were reported by Hurtgen in North America, and by Love, working in Australia. A large amount of research and investigation work has been put into trying to obtain an understanding of the problem, and into attempting to find some solutions.

Both indoor and outdoor producers have reported the problem, and it may be specific to one farm whilst neighbouring herds remain unaffected. In the northern hemisphere lowered conception rates are noticed in the period from late June through to September. Both sows and boars are affected, with sows sometimes exhibiting reduced oestrous activity and boars lacking libido, with poor semen quality. Records will show increased numbers of returns to service and repeat matings. As a result, the affected herds carry more barren sows in late autumn, with reduced numbers of sows farrowing in the months from November through to February and March, and lower numbers born. Overall, this can represent a significant financial loss to producers, but unfortunately there are no clearcut easy answers.

With outdoor herds, some infectious diseases can be ruled out by following a vaccination programme for erysipelas and parvovirus. Some herds grazing long grass in the late summer may be affected by ergot poisoning, but this is a very rare occurrence. Topping of pastures should prevent this situation from arising.

This leads to a hard look at management and service techniques. Considerable emphasis has been laid on the need to provide shades and wallows, as high ambient temperatures can be a major contributing factor to a reduction in fertility levels. Temperatures of over 35°C, which occur only very rarely in the United Kingdom, can cause temporary sterility in boars, which is an added complication.

From a management point of view it is important to check on boar-to-sow ratios, to observe and record services, to prevent boars overworking, and to pay as much attention to detail as possible. The knowledge that the later summer months are a critical period for matings can be an important factor in helping to overcome some of the problems. A thorough check should be made on feed amounts, levels, distribution and nutrient content. Are newly weaned sows in adequate condition, and are boars being fed according to their requirements? Records should show the last month, quarter, and annual feed usage figures and whether these are on target of around 1.26 tonnes per sow per year, including unserved gilts. Daylight length may have a significant effect on reproductive performance, as the outdoor system relies entirely on natural daylight. Wheeler (1986) in his paper in *The Pig Veterinary Society Proceedings* No. 18, summarises the position, stating that 'the effect of photoperiod is probably an important factor in the seasonal variations that occur independently of feed intake (between 1.10 and 1.25 tonnes per sow per year) which produces a decrease in fertility index of 7.5 per cent between the times of year when day length is constant and when it changes most rapidly.'

Feeding methods, nutrition, management, environmental conditions and disease control all have an important role to play in helping to resolve the problems of seasonal infertility. Research and investigation continue on a worldwide basis, but the veterinary consultant and day-to-day management have the largest contribution to make in finding solutions in a specific outdoor herd.

Vices

Vices in outdoor pigs are few compared to pigs housed indoors. There are some rare cases of savaging and cannibalism of newborn pigs, most often seen in gilts. This may mean removal of the offending gilt and cross-fostering of the litter. An injection of tranquilliser may be necessary. In my experience, this sort of problem rarely happens a second time around.

Stone chewing or carrying is sometimes a problem, filling up water troughs and feeders with stones. I do not know of any remedies, and in any case it is nothing more than a nuisance, and has been compared with our habit of chewing gum or tobacco!

THE DRUG AND VETERINARY STORE

Most outdoor herds will have the use of a locked office or store in which to keep medicines and vaccines. The manufacturers' recommendations should be closely followed, and some products do need refrigeration. Disposable syringes will be used for most jobs, but other syringes, needles and scalpels need sanitary storage conditions, and should be kept carefully in a store cupboard. All the small tools and equipment used for pig handling, ringing and earmarking need to be organised and controlled, to be ready for getting jobs done at the correct time.

A handy way of storing and carrying this equipment around is to use a plastic tool box. This moulded plastic container has two compartments and a handle, and the recessed groove between the compartments makes it easy to balance on the side board of the livestock trailer.

A quick glance inside the refrigerator and the medicine cupboard will reveal a good deal about the attitude and organisation of the management team. Is the refrigerator full of out-of-date vaccines, or does it hold only a few moulding sandwiches and soft drinks? Are the teeth clippers clean, and are there adequate supplies of cotton wool, assorted needles, and scalpel blades? What about the first-aid box for staff use, and have supplies been replaced? A well-organised and correctly stocked veterinary cupboard is the trademark of a well-run system, as well as providing the right tools, equipment, and medicines for use in an emergency.

Chapter Nine

RECORDING, BUDGETS AND RESULTS

RECORDING

Introduction

THE IMPORTANCE of, and need for, recording the overall performance of the outdoor herd cannot be over-emphasised. A continuous and accurate check on pig performance is essential in order to provide the necessary information for running a profitable business. Recording is only a means to an end, and any recording system should be simple to operate, and be directed towards improving pig performance and profit. Recording information on the health of the herd also falls within the overall definition.

In many herds, a whole range of data is collected that is of no particular use. Computerisation has added more categories of information, and the 'garbage in – garbage out' rule can be applied to many pig recording systems.

The recording system should be:

- Simple to operate
- Processed without delay
- Easy to analyse and interpret
- Relevant to the specific production system.

Recording for Outdoor Pig Production

Some Problem Areas
The outdoor producer has a few special problems in recording herd performance, mainly because the collection and recording of information in all weather conditions can be difficult. Paper and pen are not always immediately at hand—and may not function anyway—and a single-minded approach to recording is essential for staff working with outdoor pigs. Accuracy of data is important, as the information flowing back is only as good as the information fed in.

Most outdoor herds operate on a group system, so that there is some loss of accuracy of detail, especially at mating. Service and farrowing dates are not always known, and precise information on boar usage will not always be available. Piglet losses may be difficult to trace exactly and may have to be calculated on the difference between numbers born alive and pigs weaned. Pig counting on a daily basis may be necessary, and this area of inventory control is difficult and can be time consuming.

Identification
Quick and accurate identification of boars and sows is essential for breeding stock out of doors. This is particularly important for:

- Service records.
- Pregnancy diagnosis.
- Production information.
- Health records.

Several methods have been used including:

1. Ear notching   This is the traditional method, widely accepted for flop eared and coloured pigs, especially out of doors. It is normally carried out within a few days of birth, using specially designed pliers and a predetermined pattern, and using both ears to indicate a number. The system is permanent, and easy to read without catching the pig, but not everyone can interpret the positioning of the notches accurately, which leads to confusion. The system also involves mutilation of the ears, which may be unacceptable. Single notches can be used to denote pigs born in a particular week, or to identify pigs that are cross-fostered.

2. Ear tattooing   This process is carried out when the pigs are less than three weeks old. It is widely used in intensive systems, and done with a set of tattoo pliers with numbers that pierce the ears. A black or green paste is then rubbed into the perforations in the ear to give a long lasting and individual identification, but there is always a danger of hitting veins in the ear so that the numbers fade and blur as the pig grows. The pig must be caught and held to read the number, which is impractical under outdoor conditions. In addition, mud and dirt add to the difficulty of reading the number in the adult sow or boar.

3. Ear tags   This is the most popular method for identifying adult breeding stock. Large plastic tags can be placed in the ear at

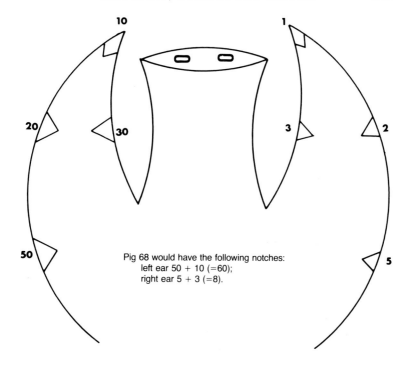

Pig 68 would have the following notches:
left ear 50 + 10 (=60);
right ear 5 + 3 (=8).

Figure 9.1   Ear notching.

delivery or service, and can be correlated with the recording system. Colour, size and type are variable, with a large range available. Some tags are already pre-numbered, others can have a number added with a special marking pen. Different colour codes can be used to indicate parity, time of entry into the herd, potential cull animals, and a wide range of production parameters. Ear tags can be lost, so tags in both ears are advisable, and lost tags should be replaced as quickly as possible. One-piece ear tags appear to have a better chance of survival, as they cannot be pulled apart. These large tags can be read comparatively easily, especially at feeding or mating, without catching or restraining the pig. They do sometimes become obscured by mud and dirt, and have to be cleaned up before they can be read.

One ingenious variation that I saw recently, developed by Alec Jones on his farm in Oxfordshire, helped to overcome this problem. He uses a large one-piece plastic tag, and notches this in the traditional manner around the edge of the tag, to give a readily visible read-out.

Choice of Recording System

Introduction
Whatever system is selected, most of the information will be collected by the outdoor staff in the field. It will be collected on a daily basis, and the job of collection may be divided amongst the team. One man may be responsible for all service records on gilts, sows and boars. Another member of the team looks after all the farrowing and rearing information until the weaners are transferred off the field. The information will be collected in a notebook or daily diary, and then transferred to a more permanent record in the office, or to a computerised system. Electronic notebooks, keyboards and logs are available, into which information can be punched, but daily notes and written records probably provide a better information base which can be stored, re-checked and referred to if necessary. Data collected by staff out on the job are called 'field records'. These will be used as an information base for office or computer records. The amount of information to be collected in the field will depend to some extent on the choice of recording system.

Manual Systems
Good manual systems have been developed over the years by concentrating on a few key figures relating to total output, the value of output, feed usage, and the cost of that feed. Manual systems do depend on experienced staff to process the field information and to turn it round fairly quickly. Accurate manual records will provide essential information for the smaller herd, but as herd size increases more time is needed to process, interpret and analyse a wide range of data. In this situation, the computerised recording systems have a great deal to offer, and a number of systems and programmes have been developed for pig production.

Computerised Systems
Computer recording is now widely used in the pig industry. The long established Pig Plan, used by the MLC, is a good example of a system based originally on manual processing, which was eventually computerised. Many organisations operate computerised recording schemes, including universities, breeding organisations, feed companies, veterinary consultants and companies specialising in com-

puter-based recording schemes for livestock production. A list of major suppliers of recording schemes and systems will be found at the end of this book.

The computerised system is able to carry out a wide range of calculations from the data presented, can process this fairly quickly, and can analyse and present results in a way which is not possible with a manual system. Hitches and delays do occur because of equipment failure, but on the whole information flow from computerised systems has improved enormously over recent years. There are two main requirements for any computerised system:

1. Entry of data should be simple and time saving, and the output easy to read and interpret.
2. The system should supply analyses that meet the customers' requirements. The customers may include staff on the pig farm, the owner/manager, the veterinary surgeon/consultant.

Such a computerised system will provide a wide range of statistics and information for the industry as a whole. The MLC *Yearbook* and the Cambridge and Exeter *Reports* are good examples of this.

Two main choices of computerised system are available, bureau or farm-based. Many organisations offer a bureau-based system, where data collected on the farm is sent away for central processing, with analysis, print-outs and results sent back to the farm on a regular basis. This is a convenient system, with fairly simple data collection. Computers are not needed on the farm or in the office, so there is no need for trained staff. In a rapidly changing technical field, the bureau has the responsibility of keeping up to date with any hardware or software that may be necessary.

Other Factors to be Considered
Breeding herd only Most outdoor producers will be concerned mainly with recording the performance of the breeding herd until the point of weaning. Litters in the field may be given only an ear notch indicating week of birth, with further identification given after transfer or sale from the breeding herd.

Reporting period Reporting periods can vary enormously, with most schemes operating on a monthly or quarterly basis. In many situations this may be too late and too long a period, and some form of weekly control is to be preferred.

Most recording schemes use a conventional calendar, but there is the alternative choice of using a 1,000 day calendar for easier calculation of key dates and events. Many outdoor herds, even with

Plate 22   Paddock gateway formed by two strips of poly tape.

Plate 23   Home-made location board used in conjunction with radial lay-out.

Plate 24   Water
Tanker used for
servicing water
drinkers in case of
hard frost.

Plate 25   Portable tool kit with syringe and notebook.

INFORMATION FLOW

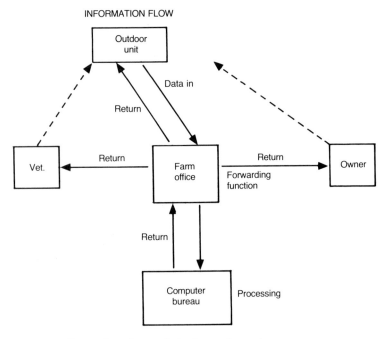

Figure 9.2   Bureau-based computerised recording system.

fully computerised systems, will use a visual display chart to keep track of the location of sows and gilts within the breeding cycle and within the paddock system on the farm.

Pigtales

The System

From a number of computerised recording systems in the United Kingdom I have selected Pigtales, which I believe is particularly suitable for the outdoor herd. Pigtales demonstrates a number of general principles which I believe are essential in a pig recording scheme. These include:

1. A bureau-based system with on-farm computer package available if required.
2. Data collected in a pocket diary, completed pages submitted weekly to a central bureau.
3. Reports, action lists and sow cards are returned weekly by post.

4. Reports are summarised quarterly, and special analyses of problem areas are available on request.
5. Reports are easy to read, produced in colour graphics and in histogram form.
6. Sows can be recorded individually as well as on a herd basis.
7. Aspects of health recording can be included in the system.
8. Targets can be set and comparisons made of actual achievements against targets.
9. The system was set up in 1979 by a group of veterinary consultants and pig producers, and has been widely used in the United Kingdom, Canada and the United States.

Data Collection
Data collection is based on the use of a small pocket diary (Figure 9.3) with the pages already ruled and prepared for entry of daily events. Animals must be identified, and events and details are entered, under simple codes, as they occur. More than one diary can be in use in one herd at the same time, and at the end of the week the completed pages are collected together and posted. Some

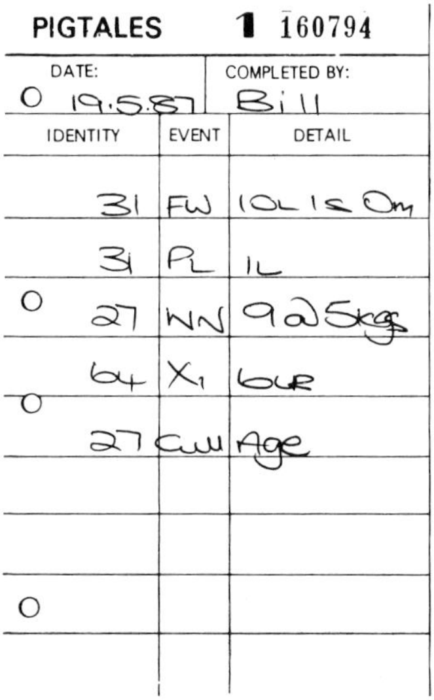

Figure 9.3 Pigtales diary card.

outdoor staff prefer to make records of daily events in their own notebook and transfer the information to the diary on a daily basis, but double handling of data can lead to more mistakes.

With an outdoor herd, not all information can be collected, but the following data should be covered:

Sow identification
Service date (if known)
Boar used (if known)
Farrowing date
Total number born alive
Total number born dead
Number transferred and fostered
Deaths in suckling
Cause of death (if known)
Weaning date
Number weaned
Sow deaths (cause if known)
Boar deaths (cause if known)
Sows culled and reasons
Boars culled and reasons.

Reports and Print-Outs
From this information, a number of reports and action lists will be prepared, including:

1. Up to five weekly reports (Figure 9.4).
2. Updated sow record cards (Figure 9.5).
3. Special analysis (Figure 9.6).

The following reports will be of special interest to the outdoor producer:

• Sow herd age structure
• Repeat service interval
• Farrowing rate cumulative to date against target
• Culls

4. Quarterly analysis (Figure 9.7).

• Efficiency report, actual and target.
• Summary—services, farrowings, losses, weanings, inventory of stock, feed/costs.

BREEDER - SERVICES CUSUM

Farm Number 015

28-SEP-86

Services since Week 27

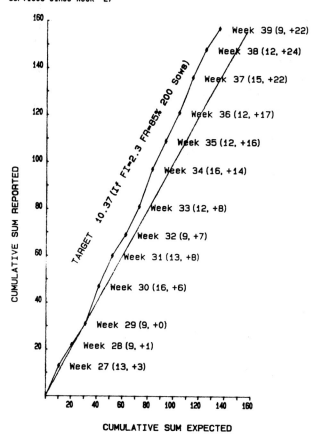

Figure 9.4   Pigtales weekly report.

PIGTALES SOW CARD

SOW G715 (X)		LAST FARROWED..... 5-JUN-86 SOW'S AGE.... 3 YRS 3 MTHS				BORN/YR.. 27.2 WEAN/YR.. 21.9		(5.2)
LITTER NUMBER	3	3	4	4	5	6	AVR	7
BOAR NAME	W33 (L/F)		W31 (L/F)		W38	W35		W43
FARROWING INTERVAL	144		161		168	147	166	
NO. OF SERVICES	1		1		1	1	1.3	1
PROBLEMS	*WW		*					
STILLBIRTHS	0		1		0	0	0.8	
MUMMIFIED	0		0		0	0	0.0	
LIVEBIRTHS	12		13		13	14	12.2	
FOSTERED ON	9	8	0	11	0	0	1.8	***CULL***
FOSTERED OFF	-12		-1	-1	-3	-4	-3.3	
PRE-WEANING DEATHS	0	-1	-1	-2	0	0	-0.7	***??***
WEANED	9	7	11	7	9	10	9.8	***AGE***
SUBSTANDARD	0		0		0		0.0	
AVERAGE BIRTH WT.	1.4		1.4		1.3	1.2	1.3	
AVERAGE WEAN.WT.	7.3	8.3	7.0	8.0	8.4	7.6	7.3	(8.2)
AGE AT WEANING	22		22		28	28	24.7	

Service Date... 7-JUL-86..........

3 Week Date....28-JUL-86....PD....

Due to Farrow..29-OCT-86..........

Date Farrowed.....................

Date Weaned.......................

Feedback

Vaccinated   Tattoo

Castrated

Iron & Tail   15

15-JUL-86

Figure 9.5   Pigtales sow card.

PRODUCTION RECORDS, BUDGETS AND FINANCIAL PLANNING

Introduction

Accurate physical performance records are only a first step in setting up a system to help monitor and control the financial aspects of an outdoor pig business. Financial records derived from the physical performance figures are another part of the information required to help control the overall economics of pig production. Forward budgets need to be prepared, based on existing track records or realistic projections. Budgets must also be compared periodically with actual achievements from both a physical and a financial point of view. Adjustments may then be needed in the technical inputs to correct imbalances in production. Capital expenditure must also be considered, and the budget will be used as a base for future cash flow requirements.

Financial Planning

Feed

This is still the major cost in pig production, and control and monitoring of feed utilisation remains a key task for the outdoor

BREEDER

SOW HERD AGE-STRUCTURE

Farm Number 666

4-DEC-86

562 Sows present on 28-NOV-86 (Av. 3.9 Cycles)

342 Sows selected with Genetic Status = LW

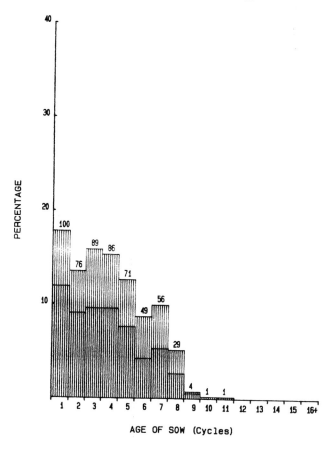

Figure 9.6   Pigtales special analysis report.

BREEDER - EFFICIENCY REPORT

Farm Number 15

22-JUL-86

Sows from 1-JUL-85 to 30-JUN-86

		PERIOD 1	PERIOD 2	
		From 1-JAN-86 To 30-JUN-86 (ACTUAL)	From 1-JUL-85 To 30-JUN-86 (ACTUAL)	(TARGET)
SERVICES	Total	272	568	541
	Repeats %	10	8	7
	Matings/Service	3.1	2.9	2.0
	Matings/Boar/Week	2.9	2.8	1.9
FARROWINGS	Total	244	484	460
	Livebirths/Litter	2688/11.0	5315/11.0	5148/11.2
	Mummified %	1	1	0
	Stillbirths %	8	9	6
	Index(Interval)	2.42(151)	2.38(153)	2.30(155)
	Born/Sow/year	26.6	26.1	25.8
LOSSES	Total	327	645	507
	Loss % Livebirths	12.2	12.1	9.9
WEANINGS	Normal (& Late)	235 (23)	475 (33)	460
	Pigs weaned/Litter	2278/ 9.7	4592/ 9.7	4641/10.1
	Late Foster % Weaned	7	5	0
	Substandard % Weaned	1	1	0
	Weaned/Sow/Year	22.6	22.6	23.2
STOCK	Sows	204	203	200
	Boars	11	11	11
	Sow/Boar Ratio	18.3	17.8	18.0
FEED	Kg/Sow & Boar/year	1174	1238	1100
	Cost/Sow & Boar/year	173.78	179.57	159.50
	Kg/Weaned pig	54.9	57.9	50.0
	Cost/Weaned pig	8.12	8.40	7.25

Figure 9.7   Pigtales quarterly analysis.

producer. Feed cost must be spread over as many weaner pigs as possible, which highlights the importance of sow productivity.

Fixed Costs
Mention has already been made of very high fixed costs in intensive systems. The outdoor producer, by his choice of system, has a lower fixed cost per breeding animal. Even so, control of these costs is important.

Inventory
Control of stock numbers plays a vital role in maintaining productivity and throughput, and helps to spread fixed costs. A shortfall in the number of productive breeding sows can lead to reduced cash flow and reduced overall profitability. The importance of keeping up sow numbers should not be underestimated in forward planning of physical or financial output.

Sales and Returns
Actual prices received for pigs in the market place have an enormous impact on profitability. Unfortunately, this is frequently beyond the control of the producer. The weaner producer is affected by fluctuations in slaughter pig prices, and has little protection against these prices in the short run. Part of the answer lies in volume (more pigs) and quality (heavier pigs with more lean meat potential).

Variation
After a period of steady improvement in the industry, with efficiency standards increasing year by year, there is still a wide variation between the best and the worst producers, in both physical performance and financial returns. The gap continues to narrow and there is a lot of room for the efficient outdoor producer to run a profitable business, mainly through lower fixed costs while maintaining a more than reasonable output level.

A Pathway to Herd Financial Planning

Figure 9.8 is taken from an excellent publication, published by the Pig Veterinary Society in 1987, entitled *Pig Health Recording, Production and Finance, A Producers' Guide*. This is a very useful reference book on various aspects of recording and financial planning for modern pig production. The diagram neatly summarises the

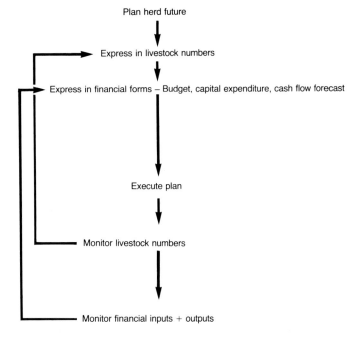

Figure 9.8   A pathway to financial planning.
Source: *Pig Health Recording, Production and Finance, A Producer's Guide*, Pig Veterinary Society, 1987.

factors to be taken into account in financial planning for pig production, and clearly illustrates the steps that should be taken.

Preparing Budgets

Carefully prepared budgets are an attempt to forecast financial performance. A budget must be prepared for a specific situation, and no two farm situations are exactly alike. It would be dangerous and misleading to generalise, as costs of inputs and outputs are subject to frequent change. Some cash flows and specimen budgets are presented later in this chapter, but should be used as guidelines only. Individual projects should have budgets and cash flows prepared, with expert financial advice which takes into account the total financial picture. Sources of specialist advice in this area include the major clearing banks, a number of financial consultancy services, and ADAS.

Financial Comparisons

Introduction
Financial planning and forecasting of any business project is essential, and well-prepared budgets should give an accurate indication of profitability. Individual farm situations vary very widely because of size, location, type of production and personal taxation. For these reasons, budgets are prepared using the financial margin system. This approach removes some of the between-farm variables, and allows calculations of margins to be made on a 'per sow' basis, or on a 'per pig produced' basis.

I have followed the definitions of financial terms used by the MLC Economics, Livestock and Marketing Services in preparing their *Pig Year Book*. These figures, and the information from the *Year Book*, are widely circulated in the industry and are used as a standard for comparison of both physical and financial information.

Margin Analysis
1. *Net output*
This can be defined as sales and credits minus purchases plus valuation change (closing valuation minus opening valuation). In practice, for the outdoor herd this means the sale or transfer of all weaners produced, and the sale or value of cull sows and cull boars. Purchased breeding stock must be accounted for, and changes in valuation are taken care of by reconciliation of opening and closing valuations of all pigs on the unit.

2. *Costs*
(a) Fixed costs
These costs are those that apply to the total herd, and do not vary according to small changes in herd size. The main costs in this category include:

Buildings and rent
Machinery and equipment
Contractors' charges
Labour
Finance charges
Stock leasing fees
Insurance
Sundries.

(b) Variable costs

These are costs that vary directly according to changes in the herd size. The main costs in this category include:

Veterinary and medication
Transport
Fuel—electricity and gas
Water charges and bedding materials
Miscellaneous small charges.

These costs will vary greatly from farm to farm and between types of production. Changes will take place from year to year as costs vary according to usage, and prices vary according to availability, supply and demand, and to inflation. A guideline to distribution of major costs for weaner producers selling weaners at a sale weight of about 30 kg is given in tables 9.1 and 9.2.

(c) Gross margin

This is calculated as follows:

Net output minus total feed costs minus other variable costs = gross margin.

This definition takes into account total sales and valuation changes, and deducts feed costs and variable costs, to give a useful comparative figure for budget and analytical purposes.

(d) Net margin

This is calculated as follows:

Gross margin minus fixed costs = net margin

This is a further refinement of gross margin which takes into account the fixed costs. It is the most valuable figure that can be calculated by margin analysis, and is the 'bottom line' produced in most comparative information.

(e) Margin over Feed

This is calculated as follows:

Net output minus total feed costs

Since feed costs account for the largest proportion of total costs, this can be a useful figure in preparing financial forecasts and in the analysis of results.

		per sow	per pig
Average number of productive sows		192	
Number of pigs/weaners sold*		10.7	
Average sale weight (kg)			29.0
Average sale value (£)			29.77
Average price per kg (p)			102.8
Output (£)	Sales—Sows & boars	16.92	1.58
	—weaners, finishers	318.64	29.69
	Other credits	1.05	0.10
	Purchases—boars, gilts	25.36	2.36
	—weaners	1.66	0.15
	Valuation change	9.11	0.85
Net output (£)		318.70	29.71
Feed costs—Sow & boar feed		89.47	8.33
—piglet feed		1.51	0.14
—rearing herd		85.03	7.92
—feeding herd		0	0
Total feed costs		176.01	16.39
Margin over feed (£)		142.69	13.32
Other variable costs	Vet & Medicine	7.67	0.71
	Transport	1.88	0.17
	Electricity & Gas	8.28	0.77
	Water	1.07	0.09
	Straw & Bedding	1.16	0.11
	Miscellaneous	4.36	0.41
Total other costs		24.42	2.26
Total variable costs (£)		200.43	18.65
Gross margin (£)		118.27	11.06
Fixed costs	Labour	42.89	3.99
	Contractor charges	0.65	0.06
	Buildings & rent	23.92	2.23
	Machinery & equipment	7.93	0.74
	Finance charges	5.35	0.50
	Stock leasing fees	0.02	0
	Insurance	1.98	0.18
	Sundries	6.33	0.59
Total fixed costs (£)		89.07	8.29
Net margin (£)		29.20	2.77

Includes pigs retained for breeding.
Variable costs (other than feed) and fixed costs are scaled up because only 66 out of 82 herds recorded variable costs and labour
50 out of 82 herds recorded fixed costs other than labour.

Source: MLC *Pigs Quarterly Report*, Dec. 1987.

Table 9.2. Costs for weaner production expressed as percentage of net output. Six months ending September 1987

	%	%
Net output		100
Costs		
Total feed costs	55.17	
Other variable costs		
Veterinary and medicines	2.38	
Transport	0.57	
Electricity and gas	2.58	
Water	0.30	
Straw and bedding	0.37	
Miscellaneous	1.38	
	7.60	
Total variable costs		62.77
Fixed costs		
Labour	13.42	
Contractor charges	0.21	
Building and rent	7.51	
Machinery and equipment	2.49	
Finance charges	1.68	
Stock leasing fees	0.00	
Insurance	0.61	
Sundries	1.98	
Total fixed costs		27.90
Net Margin		9.33

Source: MLC *Pigs Quarterly Report*, Dec. 1987.

Capital Costs

Capital Costs for Housing and Equipment
Capital costs will be the first consideration in the budget when planning a new unit or the expansion of an existing one. Guidelines only can be given, based on cost per sow place, as costs will vary for a number of reasons.

1. Size There is some indication of economy of scale when setting up larger units of around 450 to 500 breeding sows. Some costs, such as vehicles and equipment, can be shared over a larger number of sows, and by so doing the cost per sow place is reduced.

2. Type of production system Costs will clearly be higher for a herd selling weaners at 30 kg than for a herd selling three to four week old weaners directly off the field.

3. Location The type of ground and topography will affect the lay-out, and this will determine the area which may be needed for track-ways, and the amount of fencing. Proximity to services, such as water and electricity, will affect equipment costs.

4. New or second hand It may be possible to buy good quality second-hand equipment which is perfectly serviceable, and will do the job very well. I know a number of outdoor producers who have set up very practical, workmanlike units based entirely on second-hand equipment and used materials, and who achieve first-class results. A few modifications may be required, and repairs and maintenance may be higher than with new equipment, but initial capital costs are dramatically reduced. The exact degree of mechanisation will affect capital costs; it may be possible at some stages to substitute labour for equipment, particularly in the area of feed handling.

5. Integration with the arable farm Some outdoor pig producers will be able to share vehicles and equipment with the arable farm, thereby reducing capital costs.

6. Land values Calculations are based on costs of housing and equipment, and do not include the value of land used by the outdoor enterprise.

Examples of Capital Costs
Capital costs are shown for three different sizes of breeding herd. All of them carry the weaners through to 30 kg liveweight before sale or transfer. I have drawn on three different sources, and capital cost falls within the range of £150 to £180 per sow. The anticipated life of the housing, machinery and equipment will vary enormously according to design, quality, use and maintenance, but a write-off period of five years is the accepted standard.

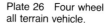

Plate 26 Four wheel all terrain vehicle.

Plate 27 Wide wheels and flotation tyres make the going easier for service vehicles.

Plate 28   Newly weaned sows enticed by a few feed cobs walk voluntarily into livestock trailer.

450 Sow Breeding Herd producing and selling weaners at 30 kg liveweight

Housing and equipment	Cost (£)
100 farrowing arks at £108 each	10,800
94 dry sow huts at £100 each	9,400
Fencing and equipment	3,575
Water supply and troughs	3,250
Tractors, vehicles and equipment	10,000
85 weaner bungalows at £375 each	31,875
	Total £68,900

Cost per sow place = £153

(Based on figures from ADAS *Booklet 2431*, revised April 1986.)

100 Sow Breeding Herd producing and selling weaners at 30 kg liveweight

Housing and equipment	Cost (£)
30 farrowing huts at £107 each	3,210
10 dry sow huts at £124 each	1,240
Fencing and equipment	500
Water supply and troughs	1,284
Tractor, vehicles and equipment	3,000
20 weaner bungalows at £350 each	7,000
Total	£16,234

Cost per sow place = £162

(Based on figures from *Outdoor Pig Production*, Masterbreeders Livestock Development, revised August 1987.)

60 Sow Breeding Herd Module selling weaners at 30 kg liveweight

Housing and equipment	Cost (£)
12 farrowing arks at £101 each	1,212
10 dry sow arks at £94 each	940
Fencing and equipment	758.50
Water supply and troughs	500
Tractor, vehicles and equipment	3,400
10 weaner bungalows at £375	3,750
Total	£10,560.50

Cost per sow place = £176.00

Based on figures supplied by Peninsular Pigs (SW) Ltd.

Gross Margin Budget for Outdoor Herds

ASSUMPTIONS

Background and methods

- This is for a typical outdoor herd operated by a tenant/manager on a light land arable farm.
- Herd size is 450 sows and 28 boars.
- Replacements are bought as maiden gilts, with 40 per cent replacement per year.
- Tested boars are replaced at a rate of 50 per cent each year.

- Purchase price: Gilts £150 per head
-                       Boars £350 per head.
- The herd is selling weaners at 30 kg liveweight.

Performance

Pigs weaned/litter	8.9
Litters/sow/year	2.30
Pigs/weaned/sow/year	20.4
Weaners/sold/sow/year	20.0
Weight at sale	30 kg liveweight
Sow feed	1.28 tonnes/sow/year
Pig feed consumption	40.8 kg per pig

Costs

Sow feed	£140 tonne
Grower feed	£180 tonne
Feed costs/pig sold	£7.34

Labour: three man team: total salary £28,000
Rent at £250 per hectare for total of 26 hectares
Capital equipment, housing and vehicles at £145 per sow = £65,250.00 depreciated over a five-year period.

	£ per sow
Total sales	
20 weaners at £30	600.00
Less replacements	15.00
Net output	585.00
Feed costs	
Sow feed	179.20
Grower feed	148.80
Total	328.00
Margin over feed	257.00
Other variable costs	
Veterinary surgeons and medicines	6.50
Water and fuel	6.50
Transport	4.50
Straw	2.0
Miscellaneous	3.50
Total	23.00

Gross margin	234.00

Fixed costs

Labour	62.22
Depreciation on housing, equipment and vehicles	29.00
Rental	20.00
Machinery operation	5.50
Insurance/sundries	3.50
	120.22

Net Margin	113.78
Gross Margin per Pig Sold	11.70
Net Margin per Pig Sold	5.68

This budget is prepared using stated assumptions. Margins will vary according to these assumptions, and sensitivities should be prepared for a number of costs and returns.

Margins per hectare   Calculations can also be made on a margin per hectare
1. *Gross margin per hectare*
Sale of 9,000 pigs at gross margin of £11.70
= £105,300 from 36 hectares
= £2,925.00 per hectare.

2. *Net margin per hectare*
Sale of 9,000 pigs at net margin of £5.68
= £51,120.00 from 36 hectares
= £1,420.00 per hectare

An article in the *Farmers Weekly* Arable Supplement (27 Feb. 1987) calculated returns per hectare on information supplied by Peninsular Pigs and estimated returns of £3930 per hectare with a stocking rate of 25 sows/hectare, and £1963 per hectare at a stocking rate of 12 sows/hectare.

RESULTS FOR OUTDOOR HERDS

Introduction

The following section includes results from outdoor breeding herds, drawn from MLC, Cambridge, and Exeter Pig Management Scheme Reports.

Table 9.3   Results for outdoor breeding herds, 1982–86†

	1982	1984	1985	1986 Top third*
Number of herds	17	35	42	14
Herd structure				
Ave no of sows & gilts	365	433	510	647
Ave no of unserved gilts	32	48	56	88
Replacements (%)	33.1	41.9	41.7	47.3
Culled sows (%)	34.7	35.9	32.5	30.2
Sow mortality (%)	2.7	2.5	2.5	2.0
Sow performance				
Litters per sow per year**	2.06	2.16	2.23	2.31
Pigs born per litter:				
alive	9.84	10.13	10.07	10.52
dead	0.66	0.61	0.71	0.77
total	10.51	10.74	10.78	11.29
Mortality of pigs born alive (%)	11.3	10.2	10.7	9.3
Pigs reared per litter	8.73	9.10	9.00	9.53
Pigs reared per sow per year**	18.0	19.7	20.0	22.0
Weight of pigs produced (kg)	10.2	7.1	5.8	5.7
Ave weaning age (days)	32	26	23	22
Feed usage				
Sow feed per sow per year (t)***	1.20	1.25	1.26	1.26
Feed per pig reared (kg):				
sow feed	73	71	71	66
piglet feed	6	2.4	0.0	0.0
total	79	73	71	66
Feed costs				
Sow feed cost per tonne (£)	139.05	155.52	135.46	133.26
Piglet feed cost per tonne (£)	240.25	340.27	—	—
Overall feed cost per tonne (£)	141.94	156.59	135.56	133.36
Sow feed cost per sow per year (£)	169	195	171	168
Feed cost per pig reared (£)	11.23	11.51	9.65	8.86

*   Top third selected on pigs reared per sow per year.
**   Per sow figures exclude unserved gilts.
***   Per sow figures include unserved gilts.
†   Year ended September.

nb   Not all outdoor herds transferred or sold pigs from the breeding herd at weaning. Outdoor herds are defined as herds which farrow outdoors.

Source: MLC *Pig Year Book*, April 1987.

MLC first reported outdoor herds in the *Pig Year Book* in 1979, when twenty herds were recorded. By 1987 the figure had risen to forty-six herds, which is by far the largest recorded sample available.

In Table 9.3 results are shown for the years 1982 to 1986, with the number of herds rising from seventeen to forty-two. Herd size increased to over five hundred on average, which is much larger than the average of recorded indoor herds. Pigs reared per sow per

Table 9.4   Results for breeding herds farrowing outdoors
(12 months ended March 1987)

	Average	Top third*
Number of herds	46	15
Ave no of sows and gilts	486	560
Ave no of unserved gilts	46	58
Ave no of productive sows	437	495
Ave no of sows per boar	16	14
% sow replacements	40.9	44.5
% sow sales and deaths	31.8	26.1
% sow mortality	2.5	2.1
% successful services	89.9	88.6
Litters per sow per year	2.23	2.35
Pigs reared per sow per year	20.2	22.6
Qty sow feed per sow per year (*t*)	1.280	1.301
Cost of sow feed per sow per year (£)	175.92	177.17
Sow feed cost per tonne (£)	137.28	136.11
Ave litter size (born alive)	10.12	10.69
Ave pigs born dead per litter	0.67	0.75
Ave litter size (alive & dead)	10.79	11.44
Ave pigs reared per litter	9.02	9.62
% piglet mortality	10.8	9.9
Qty feed per pig reared (*kg*)	71	66
Cost of feed per pig reared (£)	9.82	8.92
Qty piglet feed per pig reared (*kg*)	—	—
Cost of piglet feed per pig reared (£)	—	—
Piglet feed cost per tonne (£)	—	—
Average wt of pigs weaned (*kg*)	5.9	5.8
Overall feed cost per tonne (£)	137.35	136.27
Ave weaning age (*days*)	23	22

* Top third on the basis of pigs reared per sow per year.

Source: MLC, Pig Improvement Services, *Quarterly Data Sheet*, 87/2.

year in this period increased by 2.0 piglets, largely as a result of an improvement in litters per sow per year, from 2.06 to 2.23. There is a significant change in age of weaning, from thirty-two days in 1982 down to twenty-three days in 1986, with a steady reduction in piglet feed intake reflecting the change to the current practice of not creep feeding the early weaned outdoor litter.

Table 9.4 shows the most recent results from breeding herds farrowing outdoors. Results from the top third of producers show a larger herd size, with a narrower boar/sow ratio than average herds. An improvement in both pigs reared per litter and litters per sow per year give the top third producers an increase of about 2.4 pigs reared per sow per year above numbers for the average recorded herd. These improved results lead to a significantly lower cost of feed per pig reared.

Comparison of Outdoor Breeding Herds with Indoor Breeding Herds

Table 9.5 compares results from forty-two herds outdoors with 260 herds indoors. Herd size in the outdoor herds is double that of the indoor sample, and overall performance is very similar, with both groups weaning at twenty-three days. The indoor breeding herds rear an extra pig per sow per litter compared with the outdoor herds. Feed consumption for outdoor herds was 1.26 tonnes per year, which is 100 kg more than the average for indoor herds, but the outdoor producer is able consistently to buy feed at a lower cost per tonne than the indoor producer.

Table 9.5   Comparison of results for outdoor breeding herds and indoor breeding herds, year ended September 1986

	Outdoor breeding herds	Indoor breeding herds
Ave no of sows & gilts	510	204
Litters per sow per year*	2.23	2.26
Pigs born alive per litter	10.07	10.50
Mortality of pigs born alive (%)	10.7	11.1
Pigs reared per sow per year*	20.0	21.0
Ave weaning age (days)	23	23
Sow feed per sow per year (t)	1.26	1.16
Sow feed cost per tonne (£)	135.46	139.31

* Per sow figures exclude unserved gilts.

Source: MLC *Pig Year Book*, 1987.

Table 9.6 gives a fuller comparison of outdoor and indoor herds, and shows the top third of producers in each group. Significant differences between the two include:

• Larger herd size out of doors
• Differences in boar:sow ratios
• Lower sow mortality in outdoor herds
• The larger amount of feed fed to outdoor herds
• The lower cost of sow feed for outdoor herds
• Slightly heavier weaners produced from the outdoor system.

The top third of producers in outdoor herds compare very favourably with the top third of indoor herds, and outperform average indoor herds in almost every category.

Table 9.6   Results from outdoor and indoor herds, MLC, June 86

	Outdoor herds		Indoor herds	
	Average	Top Third	Average	Top Third
Number of herds	43	14	260	87
Ave no sows & gilts	502	667	249	235
Ave no productive sows	442	576	229	219
Ave no sows per boar	16	15	20	20
% Sow replacements	43.0	43.1	42.4	41.5
% Sow sales & deaths	31.9	27.6	39.5	39.3
% Sow mortality	2.5	1.4	3.5	2.9
% Successful services	90.3	88.5	85.6	88.3
Litters per sow per year	2.20	2.32	2.31	2.41
Pigs reared per sow per year	19.7	21.9	21.6	23.8
Qty sow feed/sow/year (t)	1.268	1.278	1.166	1.167
Cost of sow feed/sow/year (£)	172.33	168.63	167.98	170.08
Sow feed cost per tonne	135.87	131.99	144.23	145.81
Ave litter size born alive	10.02	10.35	10.44	10.92
Ave pigs born dead	0.71	0.68	0.80	0.78
Ave litter size alive & dead	10.73	11.03	11.24	11.70
Ave pigs reared per litter	8.95	9.44	9.34	9.87
% Piglet mortality	10.7	8.7	10.6	9.7
Qty feed per pig reared (kg)	73	67	59	53
Cost of feed per pig reared (£)	9.93	8.83	9.64	7.78
Qty piglet feed per pig reared (kg)	0.30	—	0.40	0.30
Cost of piglet feed per pig reared (£)	0.05	0.01	0.18	0.13
Piglet feed cost per tonne (£)	376.81	398.28	432.77	438.57
Average weight of pigs weaned (kg)	6.1	5.8	5.7	5.7
Overall feed cost per tonne (£)	135.97	132.02	146.24	147.43
Ave weaning age (days)	23	22	22	22

Results from the Cambridge Pig Management Scheme for 1986, in Table 9.7, show a small sample of outdoor and indoor herds in two categories.

Outdoor herd performance levels follow the pattern shown in previous tables, with large herds, slightly fewer pigs produced per sow per year, but with more sow feed used at a lower cost per tonne.

Costs per pig are very similar for labour and feed, but the outdoor herds have significantly lower costs for:

- Veterinary services and supplies
- Power and water
- Maintenance
- Buildings charge.

For herds selling weaners, prices received are very similar, but the margin per pig for outdoor herds is double that of indoor herds. In a difficult year the profit per pig for outdoor herds is shown as £1.95, with a loss for indoor producers of £1.68. Return on capital employed for outdoor producers selling weaners, at 12.5 per cent, is almost double that of the indoor producers in this sample of recorded herds.

Table 9.7 A comparison of outdoor[1] and indoor herds (Cambridge results)

| | All breeding herds[2] | | Herds selling weaners[3] | |
	Outdoor	Indoor	Outdoor	Indoor
Number of herds	10	99	6	31
Number of sows in herd[5]	181	141	155	142
Number of litters	387	317	342	329
Litters per sow in herd	2.15	2.25	2.21	2.31
Age at weaning (days)	33	27	29	25
Live pigs born per litter	10.4	10.4	10.7	10.4
Weaners per litter	9.0	9.1	9.4	9.2
Weaners per sow in herd	19.3	20.5	20.8	21.2
Weight of weaners	18.8 kg	18.2 kg	29.6 kg	27.5 kg
Sow feed used per sow in herd	1.41t	1.23t	1.38t	1.21t
Feed used per weaner	kg	kg	kg	kg
Sow feed	72.8	60.0	66.3	57.3
Piglet feed	18.0	18.7	40.0	39.0
Total feed	90.8	78.7	106.3	96.3
Cost of meal per tonne	£151.53	£165.53	£153.05	£170.58
Cost of feed per tonne[7]	£151.53	£165.53	£153.05	£170.58
Compounds as % of total meal	87%	64%	92%	63%

Table 9.7 (*continued*)

| | All breeding herds[2] | | Herds selling weaners[3] | |
	Outdoor	Indoor	Outdoor	Indoor
Costs and returns per pig	£	£	£	£
Feed	13.76	13.03	16.29	16.48
Labour	4.72	4.41	4.87	4.71
Other costs				
Farm transport	.37	.29	.47	.34
Vet and vet supplies	.29	.67	.34	.65
A.I. fees	.01	.07	—	.06
Power and water	.31	1.02	.14	1.07
Miscellaneous expenses	.35	.43	.46	.54
Litter	.09	.21	.06	.22
Maintenance	.20	.37	.11	.45
Equipment charge	.21	.20	.31	.23
Buildings charge	.49	1.53	.62	1.66
Pasture charge	.39	—	.56	—
Total other costs	[2.71]	[4.79]	[3.07]	[5.22]
Stock depreciation	.50	.64	.70	.59
Total costs[4]	21.69	22.87	24.93	27.00
Weaner price (net)			29.35	29.03
Margin (excl. interest)			4.42	2.03
Interest charge (at 12½%)			2.47	3.71
Profit/(loss) per pig			1.95	(1.68)
Margin per sow in herd a year			£51.79	£43.04
Return on capital			12.5%	6.8%
Capital requirements per sow			£	£
Value of sow			106	106
Share of boar's value			11	12
Buildings and equipment			187	398
Working capital			107	113
Total capital[6]			411	629

[1] Herds where sows and farrowings were mainly outdoors.
[2] All breeding herds (weaners to eight weeks of age).
[3] Mainly breeding herds selling weaners or young stores.
[4] No charge has ben included for interest on capital.
[5] Monthly average (including in-pig gilts).
[6] Excludes capital value of land.
[7] Includes other feed (mainly by-products) 'converted' to meal equivalent.

Source, Pig Management Scheme *results for 1986*, University of Cambridge.

Outdoor herds recorded over the years by Exeter University (Table 9.8) show a very similar picture to results produced by the Cambridge *Report*. This is a relatively small sample of herds, but shows some significant changes over a six year period. For outdoor herds these include:

(a) A move to earlier weaning.
(b) A steady improvement in pigs weaned per sow per year.
(c) A reduction in the amount of feed required to produce each pig.

Table 9.8   Outdoor and indoor herds (Exeter results)

Year	81–2	82–3	83–4	84–5	85–6	Indoor herds 85–6
		Outdoor herds				
Number of herds	4	4	4	5	4	31
Average number of sows	130.4	135.2	123.2	132	143	107
Average age at weaning (*days*)	42	44	35	32	27	26
Open days per litter (*days*)	20	21	27	29	27	22
Pigs born alive per litter	9.9	10.0	10.3	10.4	10.4	10.6
Pigs weaned per litter	8.8	8.9	9.1	9.1	8.8	9.3
Litters per sow per year	2.05	2.01	2.06	2.06	2.15	2.23
Pigs weaned per sow per year	18.0	17.9	18.7	18.7	19.0	20.8
Preweaning mortality (%)	11.6	11.2	11.7	12.5	14.7	11.7
Sow and weaner feed[1] (*kg*)	NA	84	70	79	71	60
per pig weaned (£)	NA	13.5	11.8	11.2	9.6	8.9
Output, costs and margin per sow						
Output (£)	502.9	464.5	635	603	515	596
Feed[1] (£)	343.9	404.5	403	381	315	363
Labour (£)	43	44.3	55	62	64	86
(*hours*)	(19.3)	(18.6)	(19.0)	(20.0)	(20.0)	(25.0)
Other direct costs (£)	29.2	29.6	20.0	28.0	36	60
Rent and rental value						
land (£)	4.3	3.8	4.0	5.0	6.0	2.0
buildings (£)	9.5	9.2	10.0	19.0	10	460
Margin (£)	73.0	−26.9	143	108	84	39
Store and weaner pigs sold:						
Liveweight (*kg*)	28.9	31.6	29.4	29.9	29.3	28.9
Price per kg liveweight (*p*)	95	79	102.9	104.2	98.2	100.7
Price per pig (£)	27.6	25.0	30.2	31.2	28.8	29.2

[1] Inclusive of boar feed.

Source: Exeter University *Pig Recording Schemes*, 1981–1986.

(d) Labour use has increased only slightly, but though the cost of this has gone up significantly, it is still lower than for indoor herds.
(e) Direct costs and building charges for outdoor herds are much lower than for indoor herds, and in 1985/6 are a major contributory factor, along with feed costs, to a doubling of the margin for the outdoor herds over indoor herds in the recording scheme.

Financial Results for Outdoor Herds

There is very little information on financial results for outdoor herds. Table 9.7, from the Cambridge *Report*, gives some information on outdoor herds selling weaners. Table 9.9, from the 1987 MLC *Pig Year Book*, provides results from a small sample of nine weaner producers, and seven outdoor breeding and feeding herds. This is less than half the total of all outdoor herds recording with MLC. Not all herds recorded variable and fixed costs in detail, so the information must be treated with caution. This is the first year that MLC have published financial results on outdoor herds, and it will take a few more years before a valid comparison can be made with a representative sample of indoor herds.

Outdoor herds recording financial information in Table 9.9 on average sold only 17.6 pigs per sow per year, well below the average for all recorded outdoor herds. In a similar way, breeding and feeding herds selling 18.4 pigs per sow per year are probably one and a half pigs below the average of all recorded outdoor herds.

The gross margin of £8.81 per pig sold by outdoor weaner producers can be compared with gross margins for all weaner producers in 1986, as shown in Table 9.10. The gross margin of £16.18 per pig sold from breeding and feeding herds can be compared with Table 9.11, which shows gross margins for breeding and feeding herds selling pigs at different liveweights.

Gross margins, although providing a good indication of financial performance, fall short of revealing the full picture. Many outdoor producers can be seen, from officially recorded figures, to be reaching very high levels of physical performance. Their output is in line with the best indoor herds, and feed costs are only marginally higher for each pig produced. Variable costs for health and fuel use are well below those of indoor herds, and fixed costs for buildings and equipment are again well below indoor herds.

Whilst there is a considerable range between individual outdoor

Table 9.9 Outdoor herds: financial results for weaner producers and breeding and feeding herds, year ended September 1986 (MLC)*

	Weaner producers	Breeding and feeding
Number of herds	9	7
Sales		
Pigs sold per sow	17.6	18.4
Ave sale weight (*kg*)**	30.4	62.8
Ave sale price per kg (*p*)		79.6
Financial results (£ per sow)		
Net output	504.86	931.90
Feed costs		
Sow	194.70	184.71
Piglet/grower/finisher	129.46	393.02
Total	324.16	577.73
Other variable costs***		
Vet & medicine	6.10	18.19
Transport	5.05	8.26
Electricity & Gas	1.04	8.75
Water	0.60	6.94
Straw & bedding	1.86	5.97
Miscellaneous	11.06	8.44
Total	25.71	56.55
Gross Margin	154.99	297.62
Fixed costs***		
Labour	62.60	96.62
Other fixed costs	56.61	88.44
Total	119.21	185.06
Net Margin	35.78	112.56
Gross margin per pig sold (£)	8.81	16.18
Net margin per pig sold (£)	2.03	6.12

*   Outdoor herds defined as those farrowing outdoors.
**   Sale weight range 51–74 kg (breeding and feeding).
*** Not all herds recorded variable and fixed costs in detail.

nb Gross and net margins are estimated using variable costs recorded by eight weaner producers and six breeding and feeding herds.

Source: MLC *Pig Year Book*, April 87.

Table 9.10 Gross Margins for weaner producers, 1977–86*

	1977	1978	1979	1980	1981	1982	1983	1984	1985	1986
Gross margin per pig (£)	3.40	7.12	5.08	7.23	9.04	9.16	5.21	10.55	12.38	10.25
Gross margins adjusted for inflation (£)	7.20	13.96	8.81	10.62	11.86	11.03	5.97	11.52	13.00	10.25
Rate of inflation (%)**	8	13	18	12	9	5	5	6	3	

* Year ended September.
** Using the General Retail Price Index.

Source: MLC *Pig Year Book*, 1987.

breeding herds, it can safely be deduced from the very high levels of physical performance and the lower cost structure that outdoor producers will have a very satisfactory return on capital invested.

Table 9.11 Gross margins for breeding and feeding herds, 1981–86*

	Gross margin per pig (£)					
	1981	1982	1983	1984	1985	1986
Sale liveweight (kg):						
50–65	11.81	14.48	7.79	14.80	17.05	14.72
65–75	13.46	16.31	8.46	17.46	18.21	16.02
75–85	15.68	19.81	10.35	20.81	20.86	18.25
85–100	17.24	23.66	12.78	24.52	23.51	20.66
Average for all breeding/ feeding herds	14.36	18.85	10.06	19.66	20.26	18.16
Average adjusted for inflation**	18.84	22.69	11.53	21.46	20.87	18.16

* Year ended September.
** Using increases in the General Retail Price Index: 9% (1981–82), 5% (1982–83), 5% (1983–84), 6% (1984–85), 3% (1985–86).

Source: MLC *Pig Year Book*, 1987.

Chapter Ten

CURRENT DEVELOPMENTS AND A FORWARD LOOK

INTRODUCTION

THERE ARE a number of interesting developments currently taking place in outdoor pig farming, which is not surprising since this section of the industry has been strongly influenced over the past ten years by a small group of successful producers. They have been innovative and have set the pace for change, building on traditional methods of outdoor pig production. Recently they have been joined by a younger generation of producers who are taking a hard look at existing systems, and who are prepared to adopt new ideas as they come along. Systems of pig production have always been influenced by individual producers who have been keen and willing to share their knowledge and experience. This chapter mentions a few developments that are of topical interest.

MANAGEMENT SYSTEMS

Electronic Sow Feeding and Indoor Service

This is really two developments rolled into one management system. Some outdoor producers were concerned about the relative lack of control over boars and sows at weaning and service, compared with indoor systems. In a group system it is difficult to feed an individual sow according to her condition and, as described earlier, more generous feeding of groups at weaning means that boars also are fed at a higher than usual daily rate, which quickly causes them to become overweight. Mating in groups can lead to inefficient use of boar power, with some sows left unserved and a higher than acceptable number of barren females. The end result is reflected in the higher overall feed consumption noted in recorded figures. Some outdoor producers have moved weaning and mating areas indoors, to make for easier control, and then put groups of sows out into paddocks after positive pregnancy testing at thirty days. This system increases labour demands and, although it may be possible to control and observe service, individual feeding of the sows remains a difficulty. The situation has been changed by the arrival of the Electronic Sow Feeding System whereby loose housed sows can be reliably and accurately fed to individual requirements.

Large barns or covered yards, with the use of lots of straw, can readily be adapted for use. Deep straw yards can be cleaned out mechanically at intervals, or lying and dunging areas can be defined, with the dung passages scraped out regularly. The total space required appears to be about 2.3 to 2.8 sq m (25–30 sq ft) per sow.

All of this fits neatly into the large arable farm situation, which usually has covered barns, produces lots of straw, can handle big bales and solid muck mechanically, and needs the muck in the arable rotation. With electronic sow feeding sows are fed individually in a feeding station, of which there are many designs and variations, although the basic principles are similar in most cases. Sows are identified at the feeding station, using a transponder attached to a collar on the neck of the sow or incorporated in an ear tag. She enters the feeding crate through a mechanically or computer operated rear gate, and is then locked in and fed a specific amount by a computer controlled mechanised dispenser. After feeding, the sow leaves the crate by a front or side exit and rejoins the main group. Sows can be kept in groups of twenty-five to thirty with access to one feeder, or larger groups, of eighty to one hundred, can share several feeding stations. The overall layout of the system is critical, and practical experience is now accumulating on an estimated two hundred or more farms using electronic sow feeding. To summarise, the ESF system:

1. Provides for individual feeding and accurate control of sow feed intake.
2. Can be integrated into existing farm based computerised recording systems.
3. Can be used in a wide range of converted buildings.
4. Fulfils most animal welfare requirements by use of straw and freedom of movement for the animals.
5. Requires a high level of management and stockmanship.
6. Needs careful training of sows and gilts to use the system properly.

7. Requires provision to be made for boars and for sick sows needing special treatment.
8. Needs reliable and robust equipment and a good follow-up service from the suppliers.
9. Has some problem areas including bullying, vulva biting and loss of collars.
10. Is still in the development stage, and not all problems of layout, choice of equipment and management methods have yet been solved.

An outdoor producer with a herd of 500 sows, holding sows and boars in a weaning/mating area for up to thirty days after first service, would need accommodation to hold all sows weaned over a five to six week period. In practice, this would mean 100 to 150 sows, and about eighteen to twenty boars. The boar/sow ratio could be adjusted back to 1:18, although catch boars may still be needed out in the paddocks. Sows could be held after weaning in groups of twenty to twenty-five, but are more likely to be in larger groups, sharing a number of feeder stations.

The total area required would be approximately 300 to 350 sq m (3,200–3,800 sq ft) a building of 24.4 × 12.2 m or 18.3 × 18.3 m (80 × 40 ft or 60 × 60 ft). Sows would go back to the outdoor paddocks in groups, the timing depending on availability of buildings and skilled labour needed to operate the system.

This is an interesting development in outdoor pig production, with a blending of new technology with the more traditional systems. For it to be economical there would need to be some saving in overall sow feed consumption, and increase in sow output, or at least no reduction. Extra costs will be incurred in converting buildings and buying the specialist equipment, as well as in providing the necessary level of supervision and management for a relatively new technique. Many producers will be watching with interest as the development is tried and tested on a number of farms up and down the country.

HOUSING AND EQUIPMENT

Producers tend to hold strong views on housing for the outdoor sow, with special attention given to the farrowing sow.

Important features that are frequently a matter of debate include shape and size of the hut and slope of the sides. Is the hut too large to keep warm in winter, or of insufficient height, allowing the larger sow to walk away with the hut on her back? Do the sloping sides provide an adequate safety zone for the new-born pigs, or should farrowing rails be fitted? Should the hut be fully insulated to provide additional warmth in winter and to keep cooler in summer? Floor or no floor?

Many new materials, which will provide strength, durability and insulation, are now coming on the market. This is leading manufacturers to reassess the more traditional materials and designs, and their ability to meet the needs of the outdoor sow both at farrowing and during gestation. Materials include fibreglass, plastics and pre-stressed box section steel sheets. These can be manufactured in the traditional shapes, or returned to variations on the 'A' frame hut. Pre-weaning mortality rates in the best outdoor units are already below 10 per cent, but the search goes on for improvements in farrowing hut design which will further reduce that figure.

FEEDING

Since feed is still the major cost of outdoor pig production there is always interest in alternative sources of feed (other than conventional compounds) and in the methods of feeding.

Recently, experimental work has been carried out at an agricultural college in the south west of England to investigate the grazing of fodder beet, with the diet balanced by a specially prepared compound fed through an electronic feeding station. Fodder beet, like all root crops, has a limited grazing season. Trials continue with a compound feed, and a balance of fodder beet and grass.

Interest continues in a range of bulk feeds, especially grass or maize silage, which could be mechanically handled on a big bale system, and be available for sow feeding all the year round.

CURRENT DEVELOPMENTS OVERSEAS

A number of producers throughout the world are very interested in the British outdoor system. France has already imported a number of maiden blue gilts from English breeding organisations, and some units have been established in Brittany. France has a climate which is rather better than that of southern England for outdoor pig production, with warm, dry summers and mild winters, and there are large areas of light sandy soils. French producers receive support from their government with low interest loans and grants for development in special areas. It seems likely that there will be an expansion of fairly large scale outdoor pig production in west and south-west France.

English style outdoor pig production is already well established in several states in the United States, using the Camborough Blue. Southern Illinois, Missouri, Kentucky, North Carolina and Georgia have reasonable climatic and soil conditions. The main problem in the more southerly states is the hot dry summers. United States producers often lack the specialist knowledge and details that make the system work, and the lack of skilled stockmanship is a major drawback. Carcase quality and fat depth, although a matter for concern, are less of a problem in the United States market. Most slaughter pigs are sold on a liveweight basis, and carcases are skinned and trimmed to produce a wide range of fresh pigmeat and processed pork products.

FORWARD LOOK

Finally, a forward look. This must, by nature, be speculative, but I have tried to take an objective view of the role and scope of outdoor pig production in the years ahead, at least until the early 1990s. Recent estimates of the number of outdoor sows put the figure at about 40–50,000, which would account for about 5 or 6 per cent of the national sow breeding herd in the United Kingdom.

Currently, outdoor pig production can be considered as a sound financial investment, but further expansion must be seen in the overall context of pig production in the United Kingdom. At the time of writing, levels of profitability in the industry are not very encouraging, but pig production is at least free from government support, and not dependent upon any subsidy. Market forces have a strong influence on the shape of the industry, and economic factors determine that only the efficient producers will survive.

The United Kingdom is self-sufficient in pork, but imports over half of its supply of bacon and ham from Denmark and Holland. The twelve EEC countries are self-sufficient in pigmeat supplies, with a marked increase in production coming from the Netherlands. A small amount of pigmeat is exported from the United Kingdom, but not enough to be an important feature of the market.

Consumption of pork has increased slightly over recent years, to a level of 13.1 kg per head per year, while bacon and ham consumption, which had been falling for a number of years, was stable

Plate 29   Group of sows waiting to enter one of three electronic sow feeding stations.

Plate 30   Weaner bungalows with slatted outdoor run.

in 1986. This overall picture means that any expanding sector of the pig industry will have to displace existing sources of supply, either domestic or foreign.

Meat quality has become a very important factor in the market. This is not just a matter of fat depth or lean meat content of the carcase. Taste, appearance and texture are all important factors for the consumer. The trend is away from fat joints and towards trimmed pork steaks, boneless trimmed chops, and lean pork mince.

One other factor in the market, which the industry cannot ignore, is the concern of many consumers about how their pigmeat is produced. This is a national issue that will not go away. and although the market for 'real meat' is at present small, it will become increasingly important.

For the outdoor producer, the market for the slaughter pig is a significant factor in maintaining his present position, or in any expansion plans. There is general agreement that the blue sow is very successful for outdoor production, and that she needs extra fat to survive a hard working life out of doors. The drawback is that her progeny tend to produce carcases that are too fat by today's standards. This is the dilemma faced by the breeding organisations, and the challenge is to produce a sow which is hardy enough for outdoor production but whose progeny will meet the market demand for quality meat.

A Role for the Duroc Breed?

The characteristics of the Duroc breed have already been discussed in an earlier chapter and, as already noted, the Duroc has been used in the United Kingdom for a number of years. There is now renewed interest in using the Duroc to replace the Saddleback in producing a crossbred female for outdoor production. The likely method is to use the Duroc boar on the Landrace sow, and a number of these females are already in production in a number of outdoor herds. We know that the Duroc crossed with European white lines has performed exceptionally well in tough environmental conditions in the United States, but as yet there is not much recorded information on performance in this country.

There is no doubt that the progeny out of a (Duroc × Landrace) sow crossed with a Large White boar will produce a leaner carcase than that from a traditional blue sow. There are also claims that the meat from Duroc and Duroc crosses has improved eating quality when compared with the white English breeds. The speculation is that the high intra-muscular fat content found in meat from the

Plate 31   Group of newly weaned outdoor pigs brought into well strawed kennels.

Plate 32   Typical straw yard system taking groups of weaners through to 35 to 45 kg liveweight.

Duroc carcase gives better taste and texture. Trials and taste panels to date have not yet shown conclusive evidence that this is in fact the case.

A number of trials are under way in Britain to examine the growth, performance, carcase merit and eating quality of purebred Durocs and first generation F_1 Duroc crosses, in comparison with conventional white breeds and crosses. Organisations involved include ADAS and AFRC. MLC are carrying out a long-term trial to provide an overall economic appraisal of the Duroc in Britain. The indications are that F_1 Duroc crosses are already being produced by a number of companies, and in the next few years will provide an alternative choice to the blue sow for the commercial outdoor producer.

Against this background, structural changes continue to take place in the industry. The trends are easy to detect, and can be summarised as follows:

(a) The change towards fewer but larger specialist units will continue.
(b) Some of the smaller herds will be replaced by larger production units, both indoors and out of doors.
(c) There is a segment of the indoor industry that was established in the 1960s and 1970s with modern intensive confinement buildings. Many of these are now at the end of a useful working life and are coming up for major renovation or replacement. In some cases cost, planning and welfare considerations will make it difficult to continue in business. These producers are unlikely to turn to a completely new system, and this may leave a gap that could be filled by outdoor pig production.
(d) Outdoor pig production may be very attractive to a number of arable farmers not already in the pig business. A cereal surplus and an EEC levy, together with government plans for set-aside and conservation, must point to some livestock project, and outdoor pigs are the most likely choice. This may be done on a wholly owned basis, but also by renting out suitable land to manager/tenants.

There are some limitations, including carcase quality which has already been mentioned, but there will be no shortage of suitable breeding stock in the immediate future. Feed and nutrition requirements are easily met, and shortage of capital is not likely to be a problem. Financial resources will certainly be available for business investment from inside or outside the farming industry.

The main limitations will be land and labour. We are back to the basic requirements of suitable land, preferably free draining sand, gravel or chalk. Local climatic conditions, topography and unit siting are major factors to be considered alongside the specific type of land. Integration with the arable farm may not be an absolutely essential factor, but is a major ingredient of success in most situations. So it is back to the land and the vital link in all pig production—the staff who look after the pigs. Their availability, skill and stockmanship are the essential ingredients to make any system work, especially the outdoor unit. At present there are not enough managers and staff to meet current needs, which is a further constraint on large scale expansion.

Many changes happen only on the fringes of the industry, but structural changes will take place in the next few years, as they have over the last few decades. Forecasts vary widely, but I believe that outdoor production will expand over the next few years, with its share of the market increased to around 10 to 12 per cent of total production.

Appendix I

Cash Flows

Two specimen cash flows have been prepared.

60 Sow Module Selling Weaners

This is based on information provided by Peninsular Pigs (SW) and includes:

1. Assumptions
2. Capital costs
3. Performance summaries
4. Cash flow for first three years.

480 Sow Outdoor Herd Selling Weaners

This is based on information provided by PIC (UK), and includes:

1. Assumptions
2. Pig flow
3. Feed usage
4. Cash flow
5. Profit and loss statement
6. Sensitivities
7. Valuations.

CASH FLOW 1—60 SOW MODULE

ASSUMPTIONS

1. Stock Input
Sixty maiden gilts (86 kg liveweight)
Six boars
    Ideally gilts should be introduced to the boars at weekly intervals and—for maximum litter size—we suggest gilts be introduced from week six following delivery.

It is suggested that, from the end of the initial stocking period a small reserve pool of gilts is set up in order to ensure a continuous farrowing programme at twelve per month.

2. Production
It is predicted that a 95 per cent farrowing rate and a 2.4 farrowing index will be achieved.

Gilt litters born alive	9.5
Second litters born alive	10.0
Third and subsequent litters	10.25

3. Overheads
Replacements The budget has allowed for the introduction of three gilts at the end of each parity from the second parity onwards. From the end of the sixth parity a higher replacement rate may be necessary.

Straw	At 0.25 tonnes/sow/year and £30 per tonne
Rent	At £240 per hectare (£100 per acre)
Stocking density	24 sows per hectare (10 sows per acre)
Labour	1/3 stockman at £8,000 per annum
Vet./Med.	At £5/sow/year

4. Feed Costs

Sow feed	At £150/tonne and 1.25 tonnes/sow/year
Weaner feed	At £190/tonne F.C.R.I.5 :1 birth to 25 kg

5. Capital Expenditure
Prices are approximate but realistic.

This cash flow forecast does not include figures relating to bank or interest charges.

Capital Costs

Initial Stocking Costs

	£	
60 Maiden gilts at £138	£8,280.00	
6 Boars at £200	1,200.00	
Total stock =	£9,480.00	£9,480.00
Equipment		
Total sow equipment	3,410.50	
10 weaner bungalows at £375.00 each	3,750.00	
Total equipment =	£7,160.50	£7,160.50
		£16,640.50
Additional optional capital expenditure		
Stock trailer (new)	£2,000.00	
Feed wagon (A frame, new)	400.00	
Tractor (second-hand)	1,000.00	
	3,400.00	3,400.00
Total capital expenditure (including vehicles)		£20,040.50

Performance Summary

Year One

Average number of sows	50
Litters born per sow per year	1.8
Born alive per sow per year	18.0
Weaned per sow per year	14.6
Pigs sold per sow per year	12.2
Tonnes sow feed/sow/year	1.25
Feed cost per finished pig (25 kg)	7.22
Average price paid per weaner	£26.50

Year Two

Average number of sows	60
Litters born per sow per year	2.4
Born alive per sow per year	24.5
Weaned per sow per year (8 per cent piglet mortality)	22.5
Sold per sow per year (2 per cent weaner mortality)	22.0
Tonnes sow feed per sow	1.25
Feed cost per weaner	7.22
Average price paid per weaner	£26.50

Cash Flow: Year One

Month	1	2	3	4	5	6	7	8	9	10	11	12
STOCK INPUT												
Gilts in	12	12	12	12	12	—	—	—	—	—	—	—
Boars in	3	3	—	—	—	—	—	—	—	—	—	—
Total sows/gilts	12	24	36	48	60	60	60	60	60	60	60	60
Total boars	3	6	6	6	6	6	6	6	6	6	6	6
PRODUCTION												
Farrowings					12	12	12	12	12	12	12	12
Average born alive					9.5	9.5	9.5	9.5	9.5	10.0	10.0	10.0
Total born alive					114	114	114	114	114	120	120	120
Mortality 8%					9	9	9	9	9	9.5	9.5	9.5
Total weaned					—	105	105	105	105	105	110.5	110.5
Total sold (2% mortality)						—	103	103	103	103	103	108
Average value £						—	26.5	26.5	26.5	26.5	26.5	26.5
CULLS												
Sows												
Boars												
Value												
TOTAL SALES	—	—	—	—	—	—	2729.5	2729.5	2729.5	2729.5	2729.5	2862

OVERHEADS												
Gilts payments	1656	1656	1656	1656	1656	—	—	—	—	—	—	—
Boar payments	600	600	—	—	—	—	—	—	—	—	—	—
Replacements gilts	—	—	—	—	—	—	—	—	—	—	—	—
Replacement boars	—	—	—	—	—	—	—	—	—	—	—	—
Straw	37.5	37.5	37.5	37.5	37.5	37.5	37.5	37.5	37.5	37.5	37.5	37.5
Rent	50	50	50	50	50	50	50	50	50	50	50	50
Labour	222	222	222	222	222	222	222	222	222	222	222	222
Vet/Med.	25	25	25	25	25	25	25	25	25	25	25	25
Misc./Maint./Water	33.5	33.5	33.5	33.5	33.5	33.5	33.5	33.5	33.5	33.5	33.5	33.5
TOTAL OVERHEADS £	2624	2624	2024	2024	2024	368	368	368	368	368	368	368
FEED COSTS												
Sow/Boar feed	212	423	656	750	988	938	938	938	938	938	938	938
Weaner feed	—	—	—	—	—	570	750	750	750	750	780	780
TOTAL FEED COSTS	212	423	656	750	988	1508	1688	1688	1688	1688	1718	1718
CAPITAL EXPENDITURES												
Farrowing arks	—	—	—	960	—	—	—	—	—	—	—	—
Fenders	—	—	—	252	—	—	—	—	—	—	—	—
Dry sow arks	940	—	—	—	—	—	—	—	—	—	—	—
Water troughs	400	—	—	—	—	—	—	—	—	—	—	—
Bungalows	—	—	—	—	3750	—	—	—	—	—	—	—
Fencing equipment etc.	858.5	—	—	—	—	—	—	—	—	—	—	—
TOTAL CAPITAL EXPENDITURE	2198.5	—	—	1212	3750	—	—	—	—	—	—	—
TOTAL COSTS	5034.5	3047	2680	3986	6762	1876	2056	2056	2056	2056*	2086	2086
TOTAL RECEIPTS	—	—	—	—	—	—	2729.5	2729.5	2729.5	2729.5	2729.5	2862
CASH FLOW	−5034.5	−8081.5	−10761.5	−14747.5	−21509.5	−23385.5	−22712	−22038.5	−21365	−20691.5	−20048	−19272

Note—Capital expenditure does not include optional costs of vehicles.

Year Two

Month	13	14	15	16	17	18	19	20	21	22	23	24
STOCK INPUT												
Gilts in	—	—	3	—	—	—	—	3	—	—	—	—
Boars in	—	—	—	—	—	—	—	—	—	—	—	—
Total Sows/Gilts	60	60	60	60	60	60	60	60	60	60	60	60
Total Boars	6	6	6	6	6	6	6	6	6	6	6	6
PRODUCTION												
Farrowings	12	12	12	12	12	12	12	12	12	12	12	12
Average born alive	10	10	10.25	10.25	10.25	10.25	10.25	10.25	10.25	10.25	10.25	10.25
Total born alive	120	120	123	123	123	123	123	123	123	123	123	123
Mortality 8%	9.5	9.5	10	10	10	10	10	10	10	10	10	10
Total weaned	110.5	110.5	110.5	113	113	113	113	113	113	113	113	113
Total sold	108	108	108	108	111	111	111	111	111	111	111	111
(2% mortality)												
Average value £	26.5	26.5	26.5	26.5	26.5	26.5	26.5	26.5	26.5	26.5	26.5	26.5
CULLS												
Sows	—	—	3	—	—	—	—	3	—	—	—	—
Boars	—	—	—	—	—	—	—	—	—	—	—	—
Value	—	—	100	—	—	—	—	100	—	—	—	—
Total Sales	2862	2862	3162	2862	2941.5	2941.5	2941.5	3241.5	2941.5	2941.5	2941.5	2941.5

OVERHEADS												
Gilts payments	—	—	—	—	—	—	—	—	—	—	—	—
Boar payments	—	—	—	—	—	—	—	—	—	—	—	—
Replacements gilts	—	—	414	—	—	—	—	—	—	—	—	—
Replacement boars	—	—	—	—	—	—	—	414	—	—	—	—
Straw	37.5	37.5	37.5	37.5	37.5	37.5	37.5	37.5	37.5	37.5	37.5	37.5
Rent	50	50	50	50	50	50	50	50	50	50	50	50
Labour	222	222	222	222	222	222	222	222	222	222	222	222
Vet/Med.	25	25	25	25	25	25	25	25	25	25	25	25
Misc./Maint./Water	33.5	33.5	33.5	33.5	33.5	33.5	33.5	33.5	33.5	33.5	33.5	33.5
TOTAL OVERHEADS	368	368	782	368	368	368	368	782	368	368	368	368
FEED COSTS												
Sow/Boar feed	938	938	938	938	938	938	938	938	938	938	938	938
Weaner feed	780	780	780	818	818	818	818	818	818	818	818	818
TOTAL FEED COSTS	1718	1718	1718	1756	1756	1756	1756	1756	1756	1756	1756	1756
CAPITAL EXPENDITURES												
Farrowing Arks												
Fenders												
Dry sow Arks												
Water troughs												
Bungalows												
Fencing equipment etc.												
TOTAL CAPITAL EXPENDITURE	—	—	—	—	—	—	—	—	—	—	—	—
TOTAL COSTS	2086	2086	2500	2124	2124	2124	2124	2538	2124	2124	2124	2124
TOTAL RECEIPTS	2862	2862	3162	2862	2941.5	2941.5	2941.5	3241.5	2941.5	2941.5	2941.5	2941.5
CASH FLOW	−18496	−17720	−17058	−16320	−15502.5	−14685	−13867.5	−13164	−12346.5	−11529	−10711.5	−9894

Year Three

Month	25	26	27	28	29	30	31	32	33	34	35	36
Total Costs	2538	2124	2124	2124	2124	2538	2124	2124	2124	2124	2538	2124
Total Receipts	3241.5	2941.5	2941.5	2941.5	2941.5	3241.5	2941.5	2941.5	2941.5	2941.5	3241.5	2941.5
Cash Flow	−9190.5	−8373	−7555.5	−6738	−5920.5	−5217	−4399.5	−3582	−2764.5	−1947	−1243.5	−426

CASH FLOW 2—480 SOW MODULE

CUSTOMER NAME   KT 480 sows OUTDOOR

Whilst every care has been taken in the preparation of this budget, neither P.I.C. nor its employees can be held responsible for any mis-statement or mis-information contained herein.

You should not place any reliance on the figures quoted but must take your own professional advice.

This Budget does not form the whole or any part of any contract between us, but is given for your guidance only.

P.I.C. Pigflow Program   PARAMETERS Page 1

CUSTOMER NAME :   KT 480 sows OUTDOOR

Parameter Values

Breeding

			Entry	Month			
Litters / sow / year	2.25	Herd Size	1	2	3	4	5
Farrowing Rate	85.55	No. of Sows	480	144	96	96	96
Born Alive Parity 1 2	10.00	No. of Boars	32	32			48
Born Alive even running	10.30						

Mortality %	%	Sales %	%	Weight	KO %	Unit p/KG Price
Sow mortality	2.50	Weaners 1	0			0.00
Piglets 0-1 month	10.50	Weaners 2	0			0.00
Piglets 1-2 month	2.00	Weaners 3	100	32		32.00
Piglets 2-3 month	0.00	Pork/Stores 4	100	0	0	0.00
Piglets 3-4 month	0.00	Bacon/Cutter 5	100	0	0	0.00
		Bacon/Cutter 6	100	0	0	0.00

Replacement Rates

		Feed				
% sows replaced 1st year	10	Weight kg >>	90			
% boars replaced	50	Feed Conversion	3.00			
% sow repl even running	40	Total feed consumed	255			
		Creep 0-1	0.00			
Breeding Herd		Grower A	7.95		FCR WNR =	1.73
Tons feed / sow / year	1.28	Grower B	18.48		10 wks	
(inc boars share)		Grower B	20.37	(2wks)		
		Finisher 3-4	81.41		Fast Growth?	
Costs of Breeding Stock		Finisher 4-5	0.00		(1=Yes)	3
		Finisher 5-6	0.00			

Initial Gilt price	150	Feed Costs		
Boar price	350	Grower A # / ton	350	
Replacement Gilts	150	Grower B # / ton	180	
Boars	350	Finisher # / ton	0	
Sow Slaughter Price	90	Breeder # / ton	135	

Deductions		Or variable Feed prices ?	
MLC / Aujesky	0.00	(0=No,1=Yes)	0
Transport / Insurance	.50		

Overdraft Rate		Credit Periods (Months)	
Annual Rate	0	Breeding Stock	2
Monthly Rate	0.00	Relpacements	2
		Feed	2

Initial Capital #   0

PARAMETERS Page 2

Labour and other Cost build - up

	Labour	Other Costs	Depreciation	Off Farm Costs	Rent
Month 1	1800	1000	600	1000	0
Month 2	1800	500	600	1000	0
Month 3	1800	500	600	1000	0
Month 4	1800	500	600	1000	0
Month 5	2400	900	600	1000	0
Month 6	2600	1000	600	1800	0
Month 7	2800	1130	600	1800	0
Month 8	2800	1130	600	1800	0
Month 9	2800	1130	600	1800	0
Month 10	2800	1130	600	1800	0
Month 11	2800	1130	600	1800	0
Month 12	2800	1130	600	1800	0

Even running assumed equal to Month 12

CUSTOMER NAME   KT 480 sows OUTDOOR

SUMMARY STATISTICS

Sow herd size	480
Pigs weaned /sow /year	20.74
Pigs sold /sow /year	20.33
Feed used /weaner	46.00
Feed cost /weaner	9.76

KT 480 sows OUTDOOR

PIC PIG FLOW PROGRAM YEAR 1

Month	1	2	3	4	5	6	7	8	9	10	11	12	TOTALS
Pigs Purchased													
Boars	32											5	37
Gilts	144	96	96	96	48							16	520
Pig Numbers													
Boars	32					4	4	4	4	4	4	4	
Maiden Gilts	144	135	138	132	77							16	666
In-Pig 0-1 months		105	105	105	105	105	105	105	105	105	105	105	
In-Pig 1-2 months			93	93	93	93	93	93	93	93	93	93	
In-Pig 2-3 months				90	90	90	90	90	90	90	90	90	
In-Pig 3-4 months					90	90	90	90	90	90	90	90	
Empty Sows						102	102	102	102	102	102	102	
Sucklers 0-1 Months						806	806	806	806	806	806	806	
Weaners 1-2 Months							789	789	789	789	789	789	
Weaners 2-3 Months								789	789	789	789	789	
Fattners 3-4 Months									0	0	0	0	
Fattners 4-5 Months										0	0	0	
Fattners 5-6 Months											0	0	
Sales													
Weaners 1							0	0	0	0	0	0	0
Weaners 2								0	0	0	0	0	0
Weaners 3									789	789	789	789	3158
Pork/Stores 4										0	0	0	0
Bacon/Cutter 5											0	0	0
Bacon/Cutter 6												0	0
Cull sows						3	3	3	3	3	15	15	45
Cull boars												5	5
Sow Deaths						1	1	1	1	1	1	1	7

KT 480 sows OUTDOOR

PIC PIG FLOW PROGRAM YEAR 2

Month	13	14	15	16	17	18	19	20	21	22	23	24	TOTALS
Pigs Purchased													
Boars				5				5				5	16
Gilts				16				16				16	192
Pig Numbers													
Boars	16	16	16	16	16	16	16	16	16	16	16	16	
Maiden Gilts	16	16	16	16	16	16	16	16	16	16	16	16	192
In-Pig 0-1 months	105	105	105	105	105	105	105	105	105	105	105	105	
In-Pig 1-2 months	93	93	93	93	93	93	93	93	93	93	93	93	
In-Pig 2-3 months	90	90	90	90	90	90	90	90	90	90	90	90	
In-Pig 3-4 months	90	90	90	90	90	90	90	90	90	90	90	90	
Empty Sows	102	102	102	102	102	102	102	102	102	102	102	102	
Sucklers 0-1 Months	806	806	806	830	830	830	830	830	830	830	830	830	
Weaners 1-2 Months	789	789	789	789	813	813	813	813	813	813	813	813	
2-3 Months	789	789	789	789	789	789	813	813	813	813	813	813	
Fatteners 3-4 Months	0	0	0	0	0	0	0	0	0	0	0	0	
4-5 Months	0	0	0	0	0	0	0	0	0	0	0	0	
5-6 Months	0	0	0	0	0	0	0	0	0	0	0	0	
Sales													
Weaners 1	0	0	0	0	0	0	0	0	0	0	0	0	
Weaners 2	0	0	0	0	0	0	0	0	0	0	0	0	
Weaners 3	789	789	789	789	789	789	813	813	813	813	813	813	9615
Pork/Stores 4	0	0	0	0	0	0	0	0	0	0	0	0	
Bacon/Cutter 5	0	0	0	0	0	0	0	0	0	0	0	0	
Bacon/Cutter 6	0	0	0	0	0	0	0	0	0	0	0	0	
Cull sows	15	15	15	15	15	15	15	15	15	15	15	15	180
Cull boars				5				5				5	16
Sow Deaths	1	1	1	1	1	1	1	1	1	1	1	1	12

KT 480 sows OUTDOOR

PIC PIG FLOW PROGRAM YEAR 3

Month	25	26	27	28	29	30	31	32	33	34	35	36	TOTALS
Pigs Purchased													
Boars				5				5				5	16
Gilts	16	16	16	16	16	16	16	16	16	16	16	16	192
Pig Numbers													
Boars													
Maiden Gilts	16	16	16	16	16	16	16	16	16	16	16	16	192
In-Pig 0-1 months	105	105	105	105	105	105	105	105	105	105	105	105	
In-Pig 1-2 months	93	93	93	93	93	93	93	93	93	93	93	93	
In-Pig 2-3 months	90	90	90	90	90	90	90	90	90	90	90	90	
In-Pig 3-4 months	90	90	90	90	90	90	90	90	90	90	90	90	
Empty Sows	102	102	102	102	102	102	102	102	102	102	102	102	
Sucklers 0-1 Months	830	830	830	830	830	830	830	830	830	830	830	830	5556
Weaners 1-2 Months	813	813	813	813	813	813	813	813	813	813	813	813	
2-3 Months	813	813	813	813	813	813	813	813	813	813	813	813	
Fatteners 3-4 Months	0	0	0	0	0	0	0	0	0	0	0	0	
4-5 Months	0	0	0	0	0	0	0	0	0	0	0	0	
5-6 Months	0	0	0	0	0	0	0	0	0	0	0	0	
Sales													
Weaners 1	0	0	0	0	0	0	0	0	0	0	0	0	0
Weaners 2	0	0	0	0	0	0	0	0	0	0	0	0	0
Weaners 3	813	813	813	813	813	813	813	813	813	813	813	813	9757
Pork/Stores 4	0	0	0	0	0	0	0	0	0	0	0	0	0
Bacon/Cutter 5	0	0	0	0	0	0	0	0	0	0	0	0	0
Bacon/Cutter 6	0	0	0	0	0	0	0	0	0	0	0	0	0
Cull sows	15	15	15	15	15	15	15	15	15	15	15	15	180
Cull boars				5				5				5	16
Sow Deaths	1	1	1	1	1	1	1	1	1	1	1	1	12

K1 480 sows OUTDOOR

SALE/FEED PRICE YEAR 1	1	2	3	4	5	6	7	8	9	10	11	12	TOTALS
Sales - Weaners 1	0												
Weaners 2	0												
Weaners 3	0												
Pork 4	0												
Bacon 5	0												
Bacon 6	0												
Feed - Creep / ton													
Grower / ton													
Finisher / ton													
Breeder / ton													

FEED USAGE YEAR 1

Month >>>>>	1	2	3	4	5	6	7	8	9	10	11	12	TOTALS
Creep Used (Tons)						0.00	4.20	6.27	6.27	6.27	6.27	6.27	35.58
COST						0	1471	2196	2196	2196	2196	2196	12451
Grower Used (Tons)							7.30	22.63	30.67	30.67	30.67	30.67	152.61
COST							1313	4074	5521	5521	5521	5521	27470
Finisher Used (Tons)									0.00	0.00	0.00	0.00	0.00
COST									0	0	0	0	0
Breeders Used (Tons)	11.52	19.20	26.88	33.58	36.44	51.63	51.63	51.63	51.63	51.63	51.63	51.63	489.01
COST	1555	2592	3629	4533	4919	6970	6970	6970	6970	6970	6970	6970	66016
TOTAL TONNAGE	11.52	19.20	26.88	33.58	36.44	51.63	63.13	80.53	88.57	88.57	88.57	88.57	677.19
COST	1555	2592	3629	4533	4919	6970	9754	13239	14686	14686	14686	14686	105337

KT 480 sows OUTDOOR

SALE/FEED PRICE YEAR 2	13	14	15	16	17	18	19	20	21	22	23	24	TOTALS
Sales - Weaners 1													
Weaners 2													
Weaners 3													
Pork													
Bacon													
Bacon													
Feed - Creep / ton													
Grower / ton													
Finisher / ton													
Breeder / ton													

FEED USAGE YEAR 2

Month >>>>>	13	14	15	16	17	18	19	20	21	22	23	24	TOTALS
Creep Used (Tons)	6.27	6.27	6.27	6.27	6.46	6.46	6.46	6.46	6.46	6.46	6.46	6.46	76.80
Cost	2196	2196	2196	2196	2262	2262	2262	2262	2262	2262	2262	2262	26073
Grower Used (Tons)	30.67	30.67	30.67	30.67	31.11	31.53	31.53	31.53	31.53	31.53	31.53	31.53	374.53
Cost	5521	5521	5521	5521	5600	5686	5686	5686	5686	5686	5686	5686	67487
Finisher Used (Tons)	0.00	0.00	0.00	0.00	0.00	0.00	0.00	0.00	0.00	0.00	0.00	0.00	0.00
Cost	0	0	0	0	0	0	0	0	0	0	0	0	0
Breeders Used (Tons)	51.63	51.63	51.63	51.63	51.63	51.63	51.63	51.63	51.63	51.63	51.63	51.63	619.52
Cost	6370	6370	6370	6370	6370	6370	6370	6370	6370	6370	6370	6370	83635
TOTAL TONNAGE	88.57	88.57	88.57	88.57	89.20	89.68	89.68	89.68	89.68	89.68	89.68	89.68	1071.24
Cost	14686	14686	14686	14686	14631	14918	14918	14918	14918	14918	14918	14918	178001

KT 480 sows OUTDOOR

SALE/FEED PRICE YEAR 3

Sales - Weaners 1
      Weaners 2
      Weaners 3
      Pork 4
      Bacon 5
      Bacon 6
Feed - Creep / ton
      Grower / ton
      Finisher / ton
      Breeder / ton

FEED USAGE YEAR 3

Month >>>>>	25	26	27	28	29	30	31	32	33	34	35	36	TOTALS
Creep Used (Tons)	6.46	6.46	6.46	6.46	6.46	6.46	6.46	6.46	6.46	6.46	6.46	6.46	77.55
COST	2262	2262	2262	2262	2262	2262	2262	2262	2262	2262	2262	2262	27143
Grower Used (Tons)	31.59	31.59	31.59	31.59	31.59	31.59	31.59	31.59	31.59	31.59	31.59	31.59	373.09
COST	5686	5686	5686	5686	5686	5686	5686	5686	5686	5686	5686	5686	68236
Finisher Used (Tons)	0.00	0.00	0.00	0.00	0.00	0.00	0.00	0.00	0.00	0.00	0.00	0.00	0.00
COST	0	0	0	0	0	0	0	0	0	0	0	0	0
Breeders Used (Tons)	51.63	51.63	51.63	51.63	51.63	51.63	51.63	51.63	51.63	51.63	51.63	51.63	619.52
COST	6370	6370	6370	6370	6370	6370	6370	6370	6370	6370	6370	6370	80635
TOTAL TONNAGE	89.68	89.68	89.68	89.68	89.68	89.68	89.68	89.68	89.68	89.68	89.68	89.68	1076.16
COST	14918	14918	14918	14918	14918	14918	14918	14918	14918	14918	14918	14918	175074

KT 400 sows OUTDOOR

CASH FLOW YEAR 1	1	2	3	4	5	6	7	8	9	10	11	12
OPENING CASH BALANCE	0											
SALES												
Weaners 1												
Weaners 2												
Weaners 3												
Pork/Stores 4							0	0	0	0	0	0
Bacon/Cutter 5								0	0	0	0	0
Bacon/Cutter 6									12433	24866	24866	24866
Cull sows						135	270	270	270	270	810	1350
Cull boars						0	0	0	0	0	0	240
TOTAL INCOME						135	270	270	12703	25136	25676	26456
FEED PURCHASES	0	1555	2592	3629	4533	4919	6370	9754	13234	14686	14686	14686
BREEDING STOCK	0	32800	14400	14400	14400	7200	0	0	0	0	0	0
Replacements						0	600	600	600	600	600	600
LABOUR	1800	1800	1800	1800	2400	2600	2800	2800	2800	2800	2800	2800
OTHER COSTS	2000	1500	1500	1500	1900	2800	2530	2530	2530	2530	2530	2530
TOTAL COSTS	3800	37635	20292	21329	23233	17519	13300	16084	15569	21016	21016	21016
CAPITAL INVESTMENT	12400	12400	12400	12400	12400	12400						
PERSONAL DRAWINGS												
CASH FLOW	-16200	-50055	-32682	-33729	-36633	-29784	-13030	-15814	-6866	4119	4659	5439
CUMULATIVE CASH FLOW	-16200	-66255	-98947	-132676	-168309	-198094	-211123	-226938	-233804	-229684	-225025	-215585
INTEREST (OVERDRAFT)	0		0			0			0			0
CLOSING BALANCE	-16200	-66255	-98947	-132676	-168309	-198094	-211123	-226938	-233804	-229684	-225025	-215585

KT 400 sows OUTDOOR

CASH FLOW YEAR 2	13	14	15	16	17	18	19	20	21	22	23	24
SALES												
Weaners 1	0	0	0	0	0	0	0	0	0	0	0	0
Weaners 2	0	0	0	0	0	0	0	0	0	0	0	0
Weaners 3	24866	24866	24866	24866	24866	24866	25238	25612	25612	25612	25612	25612
Pork/Stores 4	0	0	0	0	0	0	0	0	0	0	0	0
Bacon/Cutter 5	0	0	0	0	0	0	0	0	0	0	0	0
Bacon/Cutter 6	0	0	0	0	0	0	0	0	0	0	0	0
Cull sows	1350	1350	1350	1350	1350	1350	1350	1350	1350	1350	1350	1350
Cull boars	240	0	0	240	240	0	0	240	240	0	0	240
TOTAL INCOME	26456	26216	26216	26456	26456	26216	26589	27202	27202	26562	26562	27202
FEED PURCHASES	14686	14686	14686	14686	14686	14831	14918	14918	14918	14918	14918	14918
BREEDING STOCK	0	0	0	0	0	0	0	0	0	0	0	0
Replacements	4267	2400	2400	2400	4267	2400	2400	2400	4267	2400	2400	2400
LABOUR	2800	2800	2800	2800	2800	2800	2800	2800	2800	2800	2800	2800
OTHER COSTS	2530	2530	2530	2530	2530	2530	2530	2530	2530	2530	2530	2530
TOTAL COSTS	24683	22816	22816	22816	24683	22361	23048	23048	24915	23048	23048	23048
LOAN REPAYMENT												
PERSONAL DRAWINGS												
CASH FLOW	1773	3309	3309	3639	1773	3255	3541	4154	2287	3814	3814	4154
CUMULATIVE CASH FLOW	-217813	-214413	-211014	-207374	-205602	-202347	-198806	-194652	-192365	-188451	-184537	-180383
INTEREST (OVERDRAFT)	0	0	0	0	0	0	0	0	0	0	0	0
CLOSING BALANCE	-217813	-214413	-211014	-207374	-205602	-202347	-198806	-194652	-192365	-188451	-184537	-180383

K1 480 sows OUTDOOR

CASH FLOW YEAR 3	25	26	27	28	29	30	31	32	33	34	35	36
SALES												
Weaners 1	0	0	0	0	0	0	0	0	0	0	0	0
Weaners 2	0	0	0	0	0	0	0	0	0	0	0	0
Weaners 3	25612	25612	25612	25612	25612	25612	25612	25612	25612	25612	25612	25612
Pork/Stores 4	0	0	0	0	0	0	0	0	0	0	0	0
Bacon/Lutter 5	0	0	0	0	0	0	0	0	0	0	0	16200
Bacon/Lutter 6	0	0	0	0	0	0	0	0	0	0	0	1440
Cull sows	1350	1350	1350	1350	1350	1350	1350	1350	1350	1350	1350	1350
Cull boars	240	0	0	240	240	0	0	240	240	0	0	240
TOTAL INCOME	27202	26962	26962	27202	27202	26962	26962	27202	27202	26962	26962	27202
FEED PURCHASES	14918	14918	14918	14918	14918	14918	14918	14918	14918	14918	14918	14918
BREEDING STOCK	0	0	0	0	0	0	0	0	0	0	0	0
Replacements	4267	2400	2400	2400	4267	2400	2400	2400	4267	2400	2400	2400
LABOUR	2800	2800	2800	2800	2800	2800	2800	2800	2800	2800	2800	2800
OTHER COSTS	2930	2930	2930	2930	2930	2930	2930	2930	2930	2930	2930	2930
TOTAL COSTS	24915	23048	23048	23048	24915	23048	23048	23048	24915	23048	23048	23048
LOAN REPAYMENT												
PERSONAL DRAWINGS												
CASH FLOW	2287	3914	3914	4154	2287	3914	3914	4154	2287	3914	3914	4154
CUMULATIVE CASH FLOW	-178056	-174182	-170268	-166114	-163827	-159913	-155999	-151845	-149558	-145644	-141730	-137576
INTEREST (OVERDRAFT)			0			0			0			0
CLOSING BALANCE	-178056	-174182	-170268	-166114	-163827	-159913	-155999	-151845	-149558	-145644	-141730	-137576

Appendix II

Conversion Tables

LENGTH

METRIC

kilometre (km)	= 1,000 metres
metre (m)	
centimetre (cm)	= 0.01 metre
millimetre (mm)	= 0.001 metre
1 millimetre	= 0.0394 in
1 centimetre	= 0.394 in
1 metre	= 1.09 yd
1 kilometre	= 0.621 miles

BRITISH

1 inch (in)	
1 foot (ft)	= 12 inches
1 yard (yd)	= 3 feet
1 mile	= 1,760 yards
1 inch	= 2.54 cm
	or 25.4 mm
1 foot	= 0.30 m
1 yard	= 0.91 m
1 mile	= 1.61 km

CONVERSION FACTORS

centimetres to in	× 0.394
millimetres to in	× 0.0394
metres to ft	× 3.29
metres to yd	× 1.09
kilometres to miles	× 0.621
inches to cm	× 2.54
or mm	× 25.4
feet to m	× 0.305
yards to m	× 0.914
miles to km	× 1.61

These tables are reproduced from *Calculations for Agriculture and Horticulture*, Boatfield and Hamilton (Farming Press).

AREA

METRIC

hectare (ha)	= 10,000 square metres
square metre (m²)	
square centimetre (cm²)	= 0.0001 square metre
1 sq centimetre	= 0.16 sq in
1 sq metre	= 1.20 sq yd
1 sq metre	= 10.8 sq ft
1 hectare	= 2.47 ac

BRITISH

1 sq inch (sq in)	
1 sq foot (sq ft)	= 144 sq inches
1 sq yard (sq yd)	= 9 sq feet
1 acre (ac)	= 4,840 sq yards
1 sq inch	= 6.45 cm²
1 sq foot	= 0.093 m²
1 sq yard	= 0.836 m²
1 acre	= 4,047 m²
	or 0.405 ha

CONVERSION FACTORS

sq metres to sq ft	× 10.8
sq metres to sq yds	× 1.20
hectares to acres	× 2.47
sq feet to m²	× 0.0929
sq yards to m²	× 0.836
acres to hectares	× 0.405

VOLUME and CAPACITY

METRIC

cubic metre (m³)	= 1 kilolitre = 1,000 litres
litre (l)	
millilitre (ml)	= 1 cubic centimetre (cc)
	or 0.001 litre
100 millilitres	= 0.176 pint
1 litre	= 1.76 pints
1 kilolitre	= 220 gallons

BRITISH

1 fluid ounce (floz)	
1 pint	= 20 fl oz
1 gallon	= 8 pints
1 fluid ounce	= 28.4 ml
1 pint	= 0.568 litres
1 gallon	= 4.55 litres

CONVERSION FACTORS

litres to pints	× 1.76
litres to gallons	× 0.220
pints to litres	× 0.568
gallons to litres	× 4.55

TEMPERATURE

(°C) degree Centigrade (also called Celsius) (°F) degree Fahrenheit
Freezing point = 0°C   Freezing point = 32°F
Boiling point = 100°C   Boiling point = 212°F

Conversion

(°C × 1.8) + 32 = °F   (°F − 32) ÷ 1.8 = °C

WEIGHT

METRIC

metric tonne (tonne)	= 1,000 kilograms
kilogram (kg)	
gram (g)	= 0.001 kilogram
milligram (mg)	= 0.001 gram
1 gram	= 0.035 oz
100 grams	= 3.53 oz
1 kilogram	= 2.20 lb
1 tonne	= 2,204 lb
	or 0.984 ton

BRITISH

1 ounce (oz)	
1 pound (lb)	= 16 ounces
1 hundredweight (cwt)	= 112 pounds
1 ton	= 20 hundredweights
1 ounce	= 28.3 g
1 pound	= 454 g
	or 0.454 kg
1 hundredweight	= 50.8 kg
1 ton	= 1.016 kg
	or 1.016 tonne

CONVERSION FACTORS

grams to oz	× 0.0353
grams to lb	× 0.00220
kilograms to lb	× 2.20
kilograms to cwt	× 0.0197
tonnes to tons	× 0.984
ounces to g	× 28.3
pounds to g	× 454
pounds to kg	× 0.454
hundredweights to kg	× 50.8
hundredweights to tonnes	× 0.0508
tons to kg	× 1,016
tons to tonnes	× 1.016

Appendix III

Suppliers of Breeding Stock, Equipment and Housing for Outdoor Pig Production

ARTIFICIAL INSEMINATION
MAFF (Reading)
Masterbreeders
  (Livestock Development) Ltd
Meat and Livestock Commission
Nitrovit Pig AI Centre
Norfolk Pig Breeders

BREEDING STOCK
Accredicross Seghers Hybrid Ltd
Cotswold Pig Developments Co. Ltd
Elite Hybrids Ltd
Masterbreeders
  (Livestock Development) Ltd
Meteor Pigs Ltd
National Pig Breeders Association
National Pig Development Co. Ltd
Newsham Hybrid Pigs Ltd
Pig Health Control Association
Pig Improvement Company
Peninsular Pigs (SW) Ltd
Premier Pig Testing Co. Ltd
United Pig Breeders plc

DRY SOW HUTS
John Booth Engineering Ltd
Brackley Saw Mills Group
Challow Products (Agri) Ltd
Coulson Agricultural Oxon Ltd
GRP Coupe Forge Ltd
McVeigh Parker
Profort Farm Systems Ltd

ELECTRONIC SOW FEEDERS
Alfa Laval Agri Ltd
Elswick Bridgend Ltd
Ernest Collinson Co. Ltd
Equipment for Livestock
  Management Ltd
Gascoigne Milking Equipment Ltd
Hunday Electronics Ltd
Idento Electronics BV
Lambert Geerkens Equipment Ltd
Microware Pig Systems Ltd
Pig Rigs Farm Equipment

FARROWING HUTS
John Booth Engineering Ltd
Brackley Saw Mills Group
Challow Products (Agri) Ltd
Coulson Agricultural Oxon Ltd
GRP Coupe Forge Ltd
McVeigh Parker
Profort Farm Systems Ltd

FENCING AND EQUIPMENT
John Booth Engineering Ltd
Bramley and Wellesley
Coulson Agricultural Oxon Ltd
Gallagher Agricultural Ltd (Europe)
Harding and White Ltd
McVeigh Parker
Pig Breeders Supply Co. Ltd
Profort Farm Systems Ltd

MISCELLANEOUS SUPPLIES

Ear tags

Alfred E. Cox
Dalton Supplies Ltd
Fearing International
Masterbreeders
  (Livestock Development) Ltd
Ritchey Tagg Ltd

Management charts

Edward Holt
Ketchum
Master Breeders
  (Livestock Development) Ltd

Pregnancy testing equipment

Medata Systems Ltd

Sow feeders

Challow Products (Agric) Ltd
Coulson Agricultural Oxon Ltd
Profort Farm Systems Ltd

Used equipment

Pig Advertiser Mayfield Ltd

RECORDING SYSTEMS

AMPLAN Management Systems Ltd
BOCM Silcock Ltd
Boot HM
Dalgety Agriculture

Easicare Computer Ltd
Farmplan Computer Systems Ltd
Hylton Nomis Computer Services Ltd
Meat & Livestock Commission
Newsham Hybrid Pigs Ltd
Pigtales Ltd

TRAILERS AND TRANSPORT FOR
LIVESTOCK

Harding and White Ltd
Lambert Geerkens Ltd
Ifor Williams Trailers Ltd

WATER DRINKERS AND WALLOWS

John Booth Engineering Ltd
Challow Products (Agric) Ltd
Coulson Agriculture Oxon Ltd
McVeigh Parker
Profort Farm Systems Ltd

WEANER HOUSING

Coulson Agricultural (Oxon) Ltd
Europquip
McVeigh Parker
Pig Breeders Supply Co Ltd
Profort Farm Systems Ltd
White Tipadel

VEHICLES FOR ROUGH TERRAIN

Duffield All Terrain
Honda (UK) Ltd
Kawasaki (UK) Ltd

ADDRESS LIST

Accredicross Seghers Hybrid Ltd
Hill Farm
Deal
Kent CT14 8DN
0304 363363

Alfa Laval Agri Ltd
Oakfield
Cwmbran
Gwent
Wales NP44 7XE
063383 8071

Amplan Management Systems Ltd
Thirlby
North Yorks
0845 597 330

John Booth Engineering Ltd
Ford Anfield Industrial Estate
Ford
Nr Arundel
West Sussex
0903 716960

Brackley Saw Mills Group
Fabrications Division
Brackley
Northants NN1 35DL
0280 703401

Bramley & Wellesley Ltd
Gloucester Trading Estate
Hucclecote
Glos GL3 4XD
0452 619613

H Boot
Pig Business Services
Bleak House Farm
Aston
Nantwich
Cheshire CW5 8DS

BOCM Silcock Ltd
Basing View
Basingstoke
Hants RG21 2FG
0256 29211

Cotswold Pig Development Co
Rothwell
Lincoln LN7 BQ
047289 591

Challow Products (Agri) Ltd
Park Road
Farringdon
Oxon SN7 7BS
0367 20091

Coulson Agricultural (Oxon) Ltd
Units 9 and 10
Rectory Lane
Kingston Bagpuize
Abingdon
Oxon
0865 821042

Alfred Cox (Surgical) Ltd
Edward Road
Coulson
Surrey CR3 2XA
01 608 2131

Dalgety Agriculture Ltd
Dalgety House
The Promenade
Clifton
Bristol BS8 3NJ
0272 738981

Dalton Supplies Ltd
Nettlebed
Henley-on-Thames
Oxon
0491 641457

Duffield All Terrain
Brunel Road
Church Fields
Salisbury
Wilts SP2 7DU
0722 334369

Elite Hybrids Ltd
Lynderswood Farm
London Road
Braintree
Essex CM7 8QN
0245 360414

Ernest Collinson Co Ltd
Riverside Industrial Park
Catterall
Preston
Lancs PR3 OHP
09952 6451

Elswick Bridgend Ltd
200 Westwood Road
Stroud
Glos GL5 4ST
04536 71205

Equipment for Livestock
 Management Ltd
Great Doddington
Northants NN9 7TA
0933 2232278

Euroquip
Strawberry Hill
Newent
Glos
0531 820545

Easicare Computers Ltd
Upton House
Beeford
Driffield
East Yorks YO25 8AF
0262 88 232

Farm Plan Computer Systems Ltd
Netherton
Ross-on-Wye
Herefordshire HR9 7HZ
0989 64324

Fearing International
Brixworth
Northampton
0604 881491

GRP Coupe Forge Ltd
Boroughbridge
N Yorks
09012 2745

Gallagher Agricultural Ltd (Europe)
Curriers Close
Canley
Coventry CV4 8AW
0203 470141

Gascoigne Milking Equipment Ltd
Edison Road
Houndmills
Basingstoke
Hants RG21 2YJ
0256 463358

Harding and White Ltd
Tiebridge Farm
Houghton
Nr Stockbridge
Hants SO2 6LG
0264 810 598

Honda (UK) Ltd
Power road
Chiswick W4 5YT
01 747 1400

Holt Edward Manufacturers and
 Marketing
PO Box 79
Sutton Surrey

Hunday Electronics Ltd
Samson Close
Killingworth
Newcastle upon Tyne NE12 0DX
091 268 5828

Hylton Nomis Computer
 Services Ltd
28 The Spain
Petersfield
Hants GU32 3LA
0730 66123

Idento Electronics Ltd
PO Box 87
Chesterfield
Derbyshire S40 1YR

Kawasaki (UK) Ltd
74 Deal Avenue
Trading Estate
Slough
Berks SL1 4RZ
0735 38255

Lambert Geerkens Equipment Ltd
Henton
Nr Chinnor
Oxon OX9 4AE
0844 51391

MLC
PO Box 44
Queensway House
Bletchley MK2 EF
0908 74941

MAFF Block A
Government Offices
Coley Park
Reading
Berks RG1 6DT
0734581 222

McVeigh Parker
The Barn
Southend Farm
Bradfield
Nr Reading
Berks
0734 744777

Master Breeders
The Pig Improvement Centre
Hastoe
Tring
Herts HP23 6PJ
044 282 4211

Medata Systems Ltd
The Parade
Pagham
W Sussex PO21 4TW
0243 265528

Micro-ware Pig Systems Ltd
Low Farm
Warnfield
Wakefield
W Yorks
0924 896711

Meteor Pigs Ltd
Jackson Farm
Throcknorton Road
Nr Pershore
Worcs WR10 2PW
0386 860 128

National Pig Development Co. Ltd
Manor House
Beeford
Driffield
E Yorks YO25 8BD
0262 88426

National Pig Breeders Association
7 Rickmansworth Road
Watford
Herts WD1 7HE
0923 34377

Newsham Hybrid Pigs Ltd
Mursley Bank House
Malton N Yorks YO17 0TD
0653 697977

Nitrovit Pig AI Centre
Four Acres
Skipton Old Airfield
Sandhutton
Thirsk
N Yorks
0845 587 293

Norfolk Pig Breeding Co Ltd
AI Centre
High House Farm
Little Melton
Norwich NR9 3PE

Pig Health Control Association
Madingley
Cambridge

PIC Ltd
Fyfield Wick
Nr Abingdon
Oxon OX13 5NA
0865 820654

Pigtales Ltd
The Nursery
Burstwick
Nr Hull
North Humberside HU12 9EZ
0964 623081

Profort Farm Systems Ltd
Close Farm
Coberley
Cheltenham
Glos GL53 9QY
0242 87 482

Pig Breeders Supply Co. Ltd
Checkendon
Reading
Berks
0491 680 446

Pig Rigs Farm Equipment
The Airfield Industrial Estate
Pocklington
York YO4 2LR
0759 304850

Peninsular Pigs (SW) Ltd
Hill Corner
Berkley
Frome
Somerset BA11 5JB
0373 64713

Premier Testing Pig Co Ltd
Holbein Farm
Great Eversden
Cambridge
022 026 3416

Pig Advertiser Mayfield Ltd
18 De Braose Way
Steyning
West Sussex BN4 3FD
0903 814305

Ritchey Tagg Ltd
Fearby Road
Masham
Ripon
N Yorks HG4 4ES
0765 89541

United Pig Breeders plc
UPB House
42 High Street
Somersham
Hunts PE17 3JB
0487 840240

Ifor Williams Trailers Ltd
Cynwyd
Corwen
Clwyd
North Wales LL21 0LS
0490 2626

White Tipadel
Vallis Trading Estate
Robens Lane
Frome
Somerset
0373 645569

Appendix IV

Background Reading

GENERAL INFORMATION

Managing the Outdoor Gilt (1987), Masterbreeders (Livestock Development) Ltd.

Pigs, The Outdoor Breeding Herd (1983), Booklet 2431, MAFF.

Outdoor Pig Production. Report on an Economic Investigation by M. A. B. Boddington, School of Rural Economics and Related Studies, Wye College, Ashford, Kent (1971).

The Pig Veterinary Society Proceedings (1986), Volume 18, Parts I and II.

HOUSING AND EQUIPMENT

Housing the Pig, G. Brent (1986), Farming Press.

Environmental Needs of the Pig, Booklet 2410, MAFF.

Pig Production and Welfare, Booklet 2483, MAFF.

Farm Animal Welfare (1986), D. Sainsbury.

Pig Unit Newsletter No. 16, 'New Weaner Development', National Agriculture Centre.

MANAGEMENT

The Sow: Improving her Efficiency, P. R. English, W. J. Smith, A. McLean, Farming Press.

Control of Reproduction, ed. Cole and Foxcroft, Butterworth.

Reproduction in the Pig, Hughes and Varley.

Management of the Early Weaned Pig (1984), NAC.

FEEDING AND NUTRITION

Recent Developments in Pig Nutrition, ed. W. Haresign and D. Cole, Butterworth.

Nutrient Requirements for Pigs (1981), Agricultural Research Council.

BREEDS AND BREEDING

A History of the British Pig (1986), J. Wiseman, Duckworth.

Evolution of domesticated animals (1984), Edited I. L. Mason, Longman (Chapter 17 'The Pig', H. Epstein and M. Bichard).

New Developments in Scientific Pig Breeding, Nos. 1 to 5, Pig Improvement Company.

HEALTH

Diseases of Swine (1986), edited by A. Leman, Iowa State Press.

Pig Diseases (1986), D. J. Taylor.

Pig Veterinary Society Proceedings, T. W. Heard, MA, MB, MRCVS, Grove House, Corston, Malmesbury, Wilts SN16 0HL.

RECORDING

University of Cambridge Agricultural Economics Unit, Pig Management Scheme Annual Reports.

University of Exeter Agricultural Economics Unit, 'Pig Production in S.W. England', Annual Reports.

Pig Year Book, Meat and Livestock Commission, published annually.

FINANCIAL

Financial Management for Farmers (1986), M. F. Warren.

Farm Management Pocket Book (1986), J. Nix.

Computers on the Farm, Booklets 2456 and 2457, MAFF.

Pig Health Recording, Production and Finance: a producer's guide, produced in association with the Pig Veterinary Society.

Index

Agricultural colleges, 101
Agricultural Training Board, 101
Ancient pig keeping methods, 1
Arable station for outdoor pig
  herds, 28, 32–33
  integration with arable farm, 33–
  34
Arks, weaner, 51–52
  construction, 51–52
  management, 51–52
Artificial insemination, 92

Basic essentials, 18–31
Berkshire College of Agriculture,
  101
Boars
  acclimatisation, 77–78
  breeding policy, 82
  on delivery, 77
  entire, marketing, recent trends,
  15
  essential rules, 78
  feeding, 55
  integration and acclimatisation,
  110–111
  introduction, 77
  problems, 78
  for replacement herds, 24, 25
  purchasing, 92–93
  see also Replacement
  training, 77
  vasectomised, use, 111, 114
  procedure, 114
  weaning, 68–69
  weaning to service, 69–70
Boddington, MA, Report on
  outdoor pig production, 6

Breeding for outdoor pig-keeping,
  4–5
  policy, 24–25, 81–94
  artificial insemination, 93
  boars, 82
  cross-breeding system, 85–86
  replacement breeding stock,
  choice, 86–93
  review of breeds, 82–85
  sources of breeding stock, 27,
  93–94
  sows, suitable, 81–82
  stocks supply, recent trends, 16
  integration and
  acclimatisation, 107–114
  methods, 108–114
  veterinary advice, 104–106
Breeds for replacement, policy, 24–
  25
Brewer's grain as feedingstuff, 2
British Landrace Breed,
  background, 84–85
  boar for male line, 24–25
British Saddleback breed,
  background, 83
  as female line, 24–25
Budgets, 132–146
  see also Financial planning

Cambridge Pig Management
  Scheme, results, 151
Capital costs, 11, 140–144
  see also Costs
Cash flows, 168–186
  60-sow module, 168–176
  480-sow module, 177–186
  see also Costs: Financial planning

Cereal-producting areas and pig production, 3–4
China, outdoor pig production, 9–10
Climate, and the outdoor unit, 19
and feeding patterns, 57–58
Closed Herd Multiplier, 87, 90
Clostridium perfringens, vaccine, 114
Compound feeds, 15, 56
bulk or bag, 56
distribution, 57
intakes, 58–64
methods of feeding, 57
Computerised systems for records, 124–132
Pigtales, 128–132
Conversion tables, 188–191
Costs, capital, 11, 140–144
operating, 11–12
financial planning, 31
see also Cash flows: Financial planning
Creep feeding for outdoor herds, 13, 27–28
Cross-breeding system, 85–86

Density, stocking, 33
Developments, current, 158–167
Disease
acquired immunity, 108
cost, 103
integration and acclimatisation of stock, 107–114
methods, 108–114
Drug storage, 119–120
Dry-sow huts, 46
Duroc breed
background, 85
Landrace cross, 164
reduction of fat levels, 25
role, 164–166

Ear
notching, method, 122
tags, 16, 29, 123–124
method, 122–124
tattooing, 122

Economic Investigation of Outdoor Pig Production 1971, 6
Eighteenth century changes in pig keeping, 2–3
Electric fencing, 46–48
recent improvements, 15
Electricity supply and the outdoor unit, 19, 24
Electronic sow feeding, 158–160
Employer, requirements, 97–99
Environment and the outdoor unit, 19–24
Equipment
costs, 140–141
current and future development, 160–161
Erysipelas see Swine erysipelas
Escherichia coli vaccine, 114
Exeter University outdoor herd, results, 153–155

Farrowing
huts, 45–46
management, 72–73
gilts, 75
paddocks, 60-sow, 41–43
100-sow, 41
480-sow, 37
gilts, 37
programmes, recent trends, 13
Fat, subcutaneous, levels needed, 30
Feeding, 54–64
ad-lib, 60
amounts, 64
arable residues, 56
boars, 55
climatic conditions, 57
compound feeds, 56, 57
amounts, 58–64
compounds, advantages, 15
costs, 132–135
current and future development, 161
diet specification, 58–59
and gestation, 59
grazing-straw intake, 56
indoor sows, 54–55

in lactation 59–60
methods, 57
outdoor sows, 55
policy for outdoor herds, 27–28
sow, electronic and indoor
    service, 158–160
weaning-remating, 58
weaning to service, 69
Fencing, 46–48
    electric, 46–48
    recent improvements, 15
    problems with outdoor keeping,
        5, 7
Financial planning, 31, 132–146
    budget, gross margin, 144–146
        preparation, 136
    capital cost, 140–144
    comparisons, 137–140
    feed costs, 132–135
    financial, 154–157
    fixed costs, 137
    inventory, 135
    margin analysis, 137–140
    pathway, 135–136
    results, 146–154
    variation, 135, 138
    veterinary costs, 138
    weaner producers, *139, 140*
Finishing on farm of origin, 30
Foot problems, 116
Freezing conditions and water
    supply, 50

Gestation
    feeding during, 59,71–72
    management, 70–72
    paddocks, 60-sow, 41
        100-sow, 41
        480-sow, 36
            gilts, 37
Gilts
    feeding, 50, 60–63
        maiden, 60–61
        weaner, 61–63
    integration and acclimatisation,
        108–110
        maiden, 108–109
        weaner, 109–110

management, 73–75
    at farrowing, 75
    maiden, 73
    at service and gestation, 37,
        73–75
    weaner, 75–77
    paddocks, 37–43
    replacements, purchasing, 91–92
Grain, brewer's as feedingstuff, 2
Grassland, pig use, 35

Hampshire breed
    background, 83–84
    for outdoor production, 25
Health factors, 102–120
    cost of disease, 103
    heatstroke, 116–117
    infertility, seasonal, 118–119
    injury, 116
    integration and acclimatisation,
        107–114
    lameness, 116
    outdoor/indoor compared, 102
    parasite control, 115
    policy for outdoor herds, 25–27
    positive control, 103
    sunburn, 116–117
    vaccination programme, 107, 114
    veterinary advisor's role, 104–107
Heatstroke, 116–117
Historical aspects, 1–4
Housing, 45–46
    costs 140–141
    current and future development,
        160–161
    weaner, 50–53
        arks, 51–52
    See also Arks: Huts
Hurdles for emergencies, 49
Huts
    dry-sow, 46
    farrowing, 45–46
    See also Arks: Housing

Identification and recording, recent
    trends, 16
    ear notching, tattooing and tags,
        122–124

Immunity, acquired, 108
Indoor/outdoor compared
  employment, 99–100
  health, 102
  results, 149–154
  veterinary costs, 102
Industrial by-products as
  feedingstuff, 2–3
Industrial Revolution, effect on pig
  production, 1
Infertility, seasonal, 118–119
Injuries to pigs, 116
Intensive systems, attitudes and
  concern, 12

Lactation, feeding during, 59–60
Lameness, 116
Land requirement and stocking
  density, 33
Landrace see British Landrace
  Breed
Large White breed, background, 84
Lice, 115
Lines for replacement, policy, 24–
  25

Maiden or weaner gilts for
  replacement, 24
Management, 28–31, 65–80
  breeding stocks, stages, 67–78
  case study guidelines, 65–66
  choice, 33
  electronic sow feeding and
    indoor service, 158–160
  farrowing, 72–73
  gestation, 70–72
  gilts, 73–75
  new herd, setting up, 66–67
  weaning, 67–69
  weaning to service, 69–70
Mange, 115
Marketing, 29–31
  choice of outlets, 29
  selling, 30–31

NAC Pig Unit, Stoneleigh, 52
'Nomadic' outdoor pig units, 33

Nutrition policy for outdoor herds,
  27–28

Office facilities, 49
Outdoor pig production
  advantages, 6
  disadvantages, 5–6, 7–8
  economic investigation, 6
  overseas, 7–10
  results, 146–157
    financial, 154–157
     see also Financial planning
  traditional, 4–6
  United Kingdom, recent
    changes, 10–16

Paddocks
  layout, 35–43
    60-sow requirements, 41–43
    100-sow requirements, 37–41
    480-sow requirements, 35–37
    radial layout, 240–250 sows, 43
Parasite control, 115
Parvovirus vaccine, 114
Pig industry, technical changes, 13
Pigloo, 45–46
Pigmeat production, and EEC
  supplies, 162–164
Pigtales computerised recording
  system, 128–132
Politics, countryside, effect on pig
  production, 12

Radial paddocks, 43
Rainfall and the outdoor unit, 19
Records, 121–132
  choice of systems, 124
  computerised, 124–132
  manual, 124
  identification, recent trends, 16,
    29
  of stock, 122–124
  problems, 121–122
Rented land and outdoor herds, 28,
  33
Replacement breeding stock,
  choice, 86–93

boars, 24, 25, 92–93
closed-herd multiplier, 87
gilts, 91–92
home-bred, 87–91
maiden gilts, 24
policy, 24
purchasing parent gilts and
  boars, 91
sows, 86–93
weaner gilts, 24
*Report on an Economic
  Investigation of Outdoor Pig
  Production, 1971*, 6
Results for outdoor herds, 146–157
financial 154–157
indoor/outdoor compared, 149–
  154
see also Cash flow: Financial
  planning
Roadnight system, 4–6
advantages, 6
drawbacks, 5–6, 7–8
Rotation, arable, for outdoor pig
  herds, 28, 32–33

Saddleback *see* British Saddleback
  Breed
Selling *see* Marketing
Service paddocks
  60-sow, 41
  100-sow, 37, 40
  480-sow, 35
  gilts, 37
Services, access to paddocks, 43–44
Shade, needs, 117
Soil type and the outdoor pig unit,
  19
Sows
  farrowing, 72–73
  feeding, 54–56
    indoor, 54–55
    outdoor, 55–56
  gestation, 70–72
  paddock layouts, 36–43
    see also Paddocks
  production, 60-sow, cash flows,
    168–176

480-sow, cash flows, 177–186
replacement, 86–93
service paddocks, 60-sow, 41
  100-sow, 37, 40
  480-sow, 35, 37
weaning, 67–68
weaning to service, 69
Staff for outdoor pig production,
  28–29
indoor/outdoor compared, 99–
  100
number required, 100–101
requirements, 95–97
training, 101
Stocking density, 33
Stockmanship, essential
  requirements, 95
Store pigs, selling, 30
Straw needs, 28–29
  storage, 49
Stresnil, 68
Sty, cottager's, 2, 3
Sunburn, 116–117
Suppliers of breeding stock,
  equipment and housing,
  192–197
Swine erysipelas, 116
  vaccine, 114

Topography and the outdoor unit,
  19
Trailers, 48–49
Training, staff, 101
Trobridge Weaner Unit, 52–53

United Kingdom, outdoor
  production
  future development, 162
  recent changes, 10–16
United States of America, outdoor
  pig production, 7–9

Vaccination
  policy, 27
  programme, 107–114
Vasectomy, procedure, 114

Vehicles, 48–49
  movement of pigs, 49
  tractor, Land Rover, and trailers, 49
Veterinary factors
  costs, 138
    outdoor/indoor compared, 103
  role of veterinary adviser, 104–107
  supervision for outdoor herds, 25–26
  vaccination, 27, 107, 114

Wallows, 117
Water supply, 24, 50
  equipment, 50
  freezing conditions, 50
Weaner gilts
  feeding, 61–63

management, 75–77
for replacement, 24
Weaners
  collecting and transporting, 68–69
  housing, 50–53
    arks, 51–52
    Trobridge, 52–53
  management, 79–80
    post weaning, 79–80
  production outdoor, results, 154
  selling, 30–31
Weaning
  boars, 68–69
  earlier, recent trends, 13
  sows, 67–68
  stages, 67–69
Wire for fencing, 47–48
Worms, 115

FARMING PRESS BOOKS

Below is a sample of the wide range of agricultural and veterinary books published by Farming Press. For more information or for a free illustrated book list please contact:

Books Department, Farming Press Ltd, Wharfedale Road, Ipswich IP1 4LG, Suffolk, Great Britain.

Housing the Pig
Gerry Brent

Provides guidelines to assess proposals for investment in buildings and equipment and includes fifty detailed layouts for all classes of stock, integrated systems and ancillary services.

The Growing and Finishing Pig: Improving its Efficiency
P. R. English, S. H. Baxter, V. R. Fowler, W. J. Smith

A large, comprehensive volume which explores in detail the factors that control the efficiency of the pig from weaning to slaughter.

The Sow: Improving her Efficiency
P. R. English, W. J. Smith and A. Maclean

The best book available on the practical side of the breeding, feeding, management, health and welfare of the sow and litter.

Practical Pig Production
Keith Thornton

An excellent introduction to pig farming, full of practical advice.

TV Vet Book for Pig Farmers
The TV Vet

Over 250 pictures showing the visual signs of ailments and giving clear details about treatment and prevention.

Pig Diseases
David Taylor

A technical reference book, based on teaching notes, for the veterinary surgeon and pig unit manager. (Published by the author).

Pigmania
Emil van Beest

A collection of cartoons presenting the lighter side of porcine performance.

Confessions of an Also-ran
Peter Ashley

More light relief based on the experience of a pig-keeping partnership, manned by escapees from the City and industry.

Farm Building Construction
Maurice Barnes and Clive Mander

Practical information covering all aspects of farm building, from initial planning onwards.

Indoor Beef Production
Ron Hardy and Sam Meadowcroft

The last word on how the discipline of planned feeding and controlled environment can vastly improve production.

Farming Press also publish three monthly magazines: *Dairy Farmer, Pig Farming* and *Arable Farming*. For a specimen copy of any of these magazines please contact Farming Press at the address above.